T0013143

"In 40 brief but rich devotiona[l] helps us draw strength from [...] Although structured for the seas[...] meditations, prayers, and quotes can be savored throughout the year. Take a walk down the fresh pathways Adam opens for us—straight to the heart of our Savior. You'll be glad you did."

JANI ORTLUND, Executive Vice President,
Renewal Ministries, Tennessee, USA

"Jesus alone has the words of eternal life, and Adam's latest book will take you on a profound journey to discover their contemporary relevance. Drawing from deep wells of devotional insight, Adam weaves his soulful reflections with piercing imagery from Charles Spurgeon. A truly enriching read!"

DAN PATERSON, Apologist; Speaker;
Author, *Questioning Christianity*

"'Is Jesus real to me?' That is one of the most pressing questions of a Christian's spirituality. And in this stellar book, Adam Ramsey, with his pastor's heart and theologian's skill, takes us through the Gospel of John, where we encounter the real Jesus—the one who really is Lord and Savior, our gracious Friend, our living Redeemer. *Truly, Truly, I Say to You* will help you enjoy the real Jesus."

J. A. MEDDERS, Director of Assessment,
Acts 29; Author, *Humble Calvinism*

"This book is a delight! Adam Ramsey draws us into the heart of Christ as he reflects on the words Jesus spoke during his earthly life. Each devotion is beautifully written and leads us into greater wonder and adoration of our glorious Saviour. Read it slowly and savour the goodness of Jesus."

CAROLYN LACEY, Women's Worker, Woodgreen Church,
Worcester, UK; Author, *Extraordinary Hospitality
(for Ordinary People)*

"Since the first day I met Adam, he has consistently helped me in two ways: in digging deeper into God's word, and in discovering the riches of Christ on every page. This book is an overflow of that core part of his heart, which will call you to grow in Christ as you take your time reflecting on each word that he said. *Truly, Truly, I Say to You* is simple enough for any person to approach just as they are, yet profound enough that they will be unable to stay the same."

DAN GORRY, Lead Pastor,
C3 Currumbin, Gold Coast, Australia

"By the time I had finished this book, I felt that I had been on a journey with Adam, Charles Spurgeon and the apostle John, with all of them saying to me each day, *Look at what Jesus said here— isn't he amazing?!* Adam has written a beautiful daily devotional that wonderfully causes you to stop and mull over the words and heart of our Saviour. This book has truly stirred my affections for Jesus, and I'm excited to encourage others to get hold of a copy and go on the journey too. Thank you for this gift, Adam."

STEVE ROBINSON, Senior Pastor, Cornerstone Church
Liverpool; Director, Cornerstone Collective;
Director, Acts 29 Great Britain

Truly, Truly, I SAY TO YOU

thegoodbook
COMPANY

Truly, Truly,
I SAY TO YOU

Meditations on the Words of
Jesus from the Gospel of John

Adam Ramsey

with insights from

Charles Spurgeon

Truly, Truly, I Say to You
© Adam Ramsey, 2023

Published by:
The Good Book Company

thegoodbook.com | thegoodbook.co.uk
thegoodbook.com.au | thegoodbook.co.nz | thegoodbook.co.in

ISBN: 9781784988241 | Printed in Turkey

Cover design by Drew McCall

To Kristina,
Our Saviour smiles over you more than you know,
and he smiles through you more than you could imagine.
To me most of all.

Contents

THE FIFTH WEEK OF LENT

HOLY WEEK

EASTER

A Delightfully Brief Introduction

I am convinced that one of the primary reasons why many of us possess a middle name is so that our mother can get our attention. It is a near-universal fact of life that when the woman who brought you *into* this world throws your middle name into a sentence, you are in grave danger of her taking you *out* of this world if you don't immediately pay attention. Your middle name serves as a signal. It grabs your attention. It compels you to lean in.

Similarly, Jesus had a phrase that he used for that purpose.

"Truly, truly, I say to you..."

It's a phrase that John, the writer of John's Gospel, records Jesus using frequently throughout his teaching. Twenty-four times, to be exact. These words are a way of catching our attention, as if to say, *Hey! Listen closely here. Pay attention. Underline this.*

And yet, all of Jesus' words demand such attention. Through these pages, I want to draw your eyes and your heart to various sayings of Jesus from every chapter in John's Gospel—to zero in on a phrase and turn it around a few times in your mind. I have one goal in this book: to help you pause for a few moments each day and savour the life-renewing words of Jesus, so that they linger with you throughout the day.

Though it can be used at any time, this book is structured as a Lent devotional, for reading during the six and a half weeks leading up to Easter (beginning on Ash Wednesday, and not including Sundays). Each chapter is short: no more than five to ten minutes of reading. Each begins with a passage from John to read, which I then explore, and closes with a short prayer or reflective exercise. And then, to drive the truth of Christ's words home into your heart, I've enlisted the help of someone who has been a very precious friend to me over many years now: Charles Haddon Spurgeon.

Known as the "Prince of Preachers", Spurgeon served as pastor of the Metropolitan Tabernacle in London (the largest church in the world at the time) from 1854 to 1892, where he preached anywhere from four to ten times per week. In his spare time, he also established and led a theological college and an orphanage, provided oversight for dozens of charities, and penned somewhere in the vicinity of 150 books. His collected sermons span 63 volumes, and make up the largest set of books by a Christian author in the history of the world.

Yet it was not only the quantity of words he generated—both spoken and written—that set Spurgeon apart. He preached Christ powerfully, eloquently, vividly and repeatedly. To Spurgeon, no matter how much practical help or wisdom the sermon contained, it was not a Christian sermon until it lifted up the person and atoning work of Jesus from the Scriptures. His voice in the 19th century was gospel-preaching at its finest: illuminating the mind and lighting a fire in the heart for literally millions of people in his own day.

And it continues to be so in our day.

One of the great joys I experienced while writing this book was reading hundreds of sermons by this Prince of Preachers, and hunting there for the right words to help you feel the weight of Jesus' words. I pray that you will be encouraged through Spurgeon's Christ-exalting insight and power of speech as much as I have been.

So as you lean in to listen to Jesus each day, my prayer is that you will feel the weightiness of each word our Saviour said. He who is this very moment holding the universe together by the word of his power (Hebrews 1:3)—whose word healed the sick, raised the dead, renewed the downcast, instructed storms, commanded water, multiplied lunches, silenced demons, confounded scholars, enraged hypocrites and called the spiritually dead into the joy of fullness of life—still speaks through his word, the Bible.

And John, wanting to ensure that we understand exactly who it is that is speaking to us, begins his account of Jesus' life with an earthquake of theological eloquence:

> *"In the beginning was the Word, and the Word was with God, and the Word was God. He was in the beginning with God. All things were made through him, and without him was not any thing made that was made. In him was life, and the life was the light of men. The light shines in the darkness, and the darkness has not overcome it."*
>
> *(John 1:1-5)*

May God give us ears to hear him who speaks to us—to really hear him. As my co-author encourages us, "He bids you come to Him. His loving voice invites you to draw near. At His word press forward once again, let down the net once more, and joys unspeakable await you, surpassing all you have up to now experienced."[1] May the words of the Saviour that we explore in these pages arrest your attention and captivate your thoughts. May they refresh you even as they provoke you. May they give you life in his name.

---

1 Charles Spurgeon, "At Your Word", Sermon #1654.

CHAPTER 1

"What are you seeking?"

READ JOHN 1:35-41

*H*ave you ever considered the significance of the fact that the first words of Jesus recorded in John's account of his life are a question?

Two disciples decide to trail Jesus as he leaves the Jordan River: the first is Andrew (the brother of Peter), while the second is generally speculated to be John (the author of this narrative). On the surface, it seems relatively straightforward. Andrew and John hear John the Baptiser proclaim, *"Behold the Lamb of God!"* and begin following Jesus as he makes his way back into town. Jesus, likely hearing footsteps trailing him, turns and asks what they want.

Pause for a moment and think about that. Before we hear Jesus giving a single directive or instruction, he asks a question that gets right to the heart. Their hearts. *What are you seeking?* For when God asks a question, he is not seeking information unknown to *himself.* He is helping us to see *ourselves,* in light of who he is.

When Adam and Eve were hiding from God in the shame of their first sin, and God asked, *"Where are you?"* (Genesis 3:9), it wasn't because he was unaware of their geographic location. It was because they were unaware of the full impact of the new spiritual location that their rebellion had put them in.

When God asked Job, *"Where were you when I laid the foundation of the earth?"* (Job 38:4), it wasn't because he was unsure whether or not Job had existed eternally as a witness to the events of Genesis 1. The question wasn't for God's sake but for Job's.

"What are you seeking?" (John 1:38)

Jesus did not ask for his own sake but for Andrew and John's. And for ours. Jesus desires our *desires*. He wants the meaning-seeking, beauty-desiring, satisfaction-questing centre of who we are: our hearts. And so he asks, *"What are you seeking?"* We humans are seeking-creatures, hunting for fulfilment. We can't help it. For our desires, our identity, and our direction are all woven together. Or, as author James K.A. Smith puts it, *we are what we want*. Smith writes, "Our wants and longings and desires are at the core of our identity, the wellspring from which our actions and behavior flow".[2] As it turns out, Jesus' question penetrates to the core of who we are. And it changes John's life.

First words and last words have a way of staying with us. Years later, as John wrote this account near the end of his life, he could still remember the first words Jesus ever spoke to him. It was only four words, spoken on a dusty wilderness road somewhere near the Jordan River. But the soul-piercing simplicity of those words stayed with John through the decades of his long life, because they redirected the trajectory of that life.

The scene closes with Andrew going to tell his brother Peter, "We have found the Messiah". For these first disciples, the question that probed at a *what* was answered with a *who*.

---

2 James K.A. Smith, *You Are What You Love: The Spiritual Power of Habit* (Brazos Press, 2016), p 2.

Because that's what real Christianity is: a constant reorienting of everything in our lives around the person and work of Jesus.

What do your present habits reveal about your desires?

What do your present worries and your prayers reveal about your longings?

What does your present way of speaking, to others and to yourself, reveal about your heart?

As you make your way through these short devotionals on the words of Jesus, return to his question, which turns out to be an invitation: *"What are you seeking?"* Alexander Maclaren, a Scottish Baptist minister writing a little over a century ago, helps us see the answer:

> *"Let me tell you what you are seeking, whether you know it or not. You are seeking for rest for your heart, a home for your spirits; you are seeking for perfect truth for your understandings, perfect beauty for your affections, perfect goodness for your conscience. You are seeking for all these three, gathered into one white beam of light, and you are seeking for it all in a Person. Many of you do not know this, and so you go hunting in all manner of impossible places for that which you can only find in one. To the question, 'What seek ye?' the deepest of all answers, the only real answer, is, 'My soul thirsteth for God, for the living God.' If you know that, you know where to look for what you need!"* [3]

You know where to look for what you need! It is to the promised one, whom the Old Testament anticipates and the New Testament reveals. It is to the Son of God, of whom John the Baptiser preached and Andrew the disciple gave witness: *"Behold the Lamb of God! ... We have found the Messiah."*

---

3 Alexander Maclaren, *Expositions of Holy Scripture: St John Chapters I-XIV* (Eerdmans, 1938), p 54.

PRAY

Lord, there are a thousand things competing for my attention today. Some are important; many are not. But I don't want a single one of them to obstruct my view of you. Help me not lose sight of you today. I want to follow you more faithfully. I want to know you more deeply. I want to want you more. Amen.

"'What is it that you seek?' ... He puts the same question to you this morning—'What seek you?' Are you seeking pardon? You shall find it in Me. Are you seeking peace? I will give you rest. Are you seeking purity? I will take away your sin, a new heart will I give you and a right spirit will I put within you. What are you seeking? Some solid resting place for your soul upon earth, and a glorious hope for yourself in heaven? Whatever you seek, it is here ... O my dear friend, if you would but come and see Christ, if by humble earnest prayer you would give your heart up to Him, and then trust in Him implicitly to be your guide, you would never lament the decision."

Charles Spurgeon, "The First Five Disciples", Sermon #570

CHAPTER 2

"Follow me"

READ JOHN 1:43-45

*T*here are a lot of reasons why I love the movie *Braveheart*. But one in particular is the contrast of leadership styles between the Scottish freedom fighter William Wallace and the English king and generals. Both call armies to follow them into battle. Both give orders. Both demand sacrifice and self-denial. The difference between them, however, is one of location. The English king gives orders from the safety of the back. Wallace leads from the front. The former leads with instructions, but the latter leads by example. And at the risk of stating the obvious, to properly *follow* another requires being able to see their back, not merely hear their voice.

Jesus is the most trustworthy leader in the history of the world. Life under the rule of Jesus is not merely instructed; it is modelled. He is both our goal and our guide: a glorious King as well as our perfect example. John wants us to see that when Jesus calls us to follow him, he is calling for an all-of-life exchange: all that we are for all that he is. *Follow me.*

Follow me. Interestingly, no reason is given to Philip for *why* he ought to follow. No enticement or reward is offered. The sermon is short—only two words in total—but the message pierces Philip's heart and gets to the core of what real

Christianity is: drawing near to Jesus, over and over and over again. The sum of which is a life that follows him, walks with him and gradually yet increasingly reflects him.

Philip sees in Jesus a leader who is both trustworthy and worthy of his immediate devotion and allegiance. No one can place conditions or limits on the leadership of Jesus and with integrity claim to be one of his followers; for the moment we say, "Ok Jesus, I'll follow you *if* you bless me, *if* you make my career successful, *if* you make me healthy, *if* you don't mess with this part of my life, *if* I can retain some sovereignty over my life", we are actually confessing that there are created realities more worthy, more satisfying and more important to us than Jesus.

Which is idolatry.

Which is, you know, really bad.

As Timothy Keller points out, whatever is "on the other side of that *if* is your real master, your real goal. But Jesus will not be a means to an end; he will not be used. If he calls you to follow him, *he* must be the goal."[4]

Christianity is not "Jesus, I'll follow you if you improve my life" but "Jesus, I'll follow you because you are better than life". He is our goal.

Jesus later said to his disciples, "If anyone would come after me, let him deny himself and take up his cross daily and follow me. For whoever would save his life will lose it, but whoever loses his life for my sake will save it" (Luke 9:23-24).

In other words, the only thing in all the world more costly than following Jesus... is not. Hold on to your life and you'll choke that life away. Release your life into the hands of Jesus by dying to your need to call the shots and you'll find more than everything you were ever looking for. It is

---

4 Timothy Keller, *King's Cross: Understanding the Life and Death of the Son of God* (Hodder & Stoughton, 2011), p 19.

counterintuitive, but God has ordained freedom to come through surrender and life to come through dying.

In this way, following Jesus may be hard, but it's not complicated. In fact, all that is required by the two-word sermon of Jesus is a two-word response:

Yes, Lord.

Each day. Every day.
Yes, Lord.

Come to me. *Yes, Lord.*
Learn from me. *Yes, Lord.*
Trust me. *Yes, Lord.*
Do not be anxious. *Yes, Lord.*
Love one another as I have loved you. *Yes, Lord.*
Love your enemies. *Yes, Lord.*
Go make disciples. *Yes, Lord.*
Follow me. *Yes, Lord.*

Make no mistake: the loving leadership of Jesus in this life will include both green pastures that restore us and dark valleys that trouble us (Psalm 23:2-4). But neither the absence of the former nor the presence of the latter means that he has abandoned us (v 5). And that is enough. For the command of Jesus to follow him is infused with his promise, "I will never leave you nor forsake you" (Hebrews 13:5). Is there any part of your life where you've been keeping Jesus at arm's length? Turn to him again, go to him again and say, "Yes, Lord. You're leading. I'm following. Let's go."

After all, who in all the world is more worthy of your devotion, your obedience, your trust, your life and even your death than Jesus?

PRAY

Jesus, whatever you call me to, wherever you lead me, whenever you desire me to, teach my heart to respond, "Yes, Lord".

"Christ has marked His sheep on their feet as well as their ears. They follow Him; they are gently led, not harshly driven. They follow Him as the Captain of their Salvation; they trust in the power of His arm to clear the way for them. All their trust on Him is abiding; they lean all their hope on Him; they follow Him as their teacher ... Has Christ said it? It is enough! ... Happiest of all the happy are they who see the footprint—the print of that foot that once was pierced with the nail—and put their foot down where He placed it, and then again, in the same mark, follow where He trod, till they climb at last to the throne!"

Charles Spurgeon, "The Sheep and Their Shepherd", Sermon #995

CHAPTER 3

"My hour has not yet come"

READ JOHN 2:1-11

*T*here were a number of remarkable changes that took place in the story of Jesus' first miraculous sign at a wedding in Cana. He changed ordinary water into top-shelf wine—somewhere in the vicinity of 700 to 900 bottles by our standards—with little more than a few directions to the servants. He changed an abundance of shame, which would have fallen on the groom and his family, into an abundance of joy. In this culture, wine was more than a beverage; it was representative of celebration and joy—so much so that one contemporary rabbinic saying went, "Without wine, there is no joy". Jesus even changed the relational dynamic with his mother, addressing her in the more formal manner ("Woman") rather than as "Mother". From this time onward, Mary would relate to Jesus primarily as a disciple. "She, like every other person," writes New Testament scholar D.A. Carson, "must [now] come to him as to the promised Messiah, the Lamb of God who takes away the sin of the world".[5]

Yet interestingly, the greatest change that weighed on the mind of Jesus, even here at a wedding, was the change of

---

5 D. A. Carson, *The Gospel According to John* (Inter-Varsity Press, 1991), p 171.

status that he had come to bring between the holy God and sinful humanity: the change that he knew he would literally die to bring.

Jesus said to Mary, *"My hour has not yet come"* (John 2:4).

It is the first of over a dozen times in John's Gospel that Jesus would mention "his hour". The hour on his mind was the hour of his sacrifice. And the closer he moved towards this sacred hour—the hour when he would die as a willing substitute, the innocent one in place of the guilty in order to reconcile us to God—the more he spoke of it. In other words, Jesus knew exactly why he had come. He lived with an intense intentionality towards his final hour. He obeyed the Father perfectly. He walked unwaveringly towards the cross.

Towards the hour of atonement.
Towards the hour of your justification.
Towards the hour of your forgiveness.

Have you ever considered that the hour Jesus thought of the most was the hour when he would bring you home?

On the cross, the greatest change of all took place: Jesus wore our unrighteousness, and in exchange, clothed all who believe with his own righteousness. The apostle Paul describes our new reality with his famous pronouncement in Romans 8:1, declaring, "There is therefore now no condemnation for those who are in Christ Jesus". Why are Christians a rejoicing people? Because our God is a redeeming God.

Perhaps at the wedding of an anonymous couple in Cana, as Jesus thought of "his hour," he thought of what lay in the future on the other side of his sacrifice: his own wedding— what John would later describe in Revelation 19:9 as "the marriage supper of the Lamb", the wedding that every human wedding points to, in the same way that a shadow points to the reality. You see, the climax of human history is a wedding. The greatest celebration that all of heaven and earth will behold is still ahead of us, when the redeemed people of God—the bride of Christ—are eternally united with him. Where the shame of sin is forever in the rear-view mirror, and joy, like new wine, flows in abundance.

Rewind to the joyful hustle and bustle of that wedding in Cana. In that moment, Jesus' hour had "not yet come". But it would come. And when it did, Jesus did not shy away from it. And because Jesus did not change course as he journeyed towards the cross, your course has been changed from eternal death to eternal life. And according to Paul, that is a future that no devil or difficulty in this universe can separate you from (Romans 8:38-39).

From the beginning, Jesus knew why he had come. He lived to die. He walked towards the hour of his death. But then he walked *through* it, onward through the grave and into resurrection life, which he intends to share for ever with you.

PRAY

Lord, even greater than making water into wine is the miracle in which you made me a Christian. Thank you for changing me. Thank you for all you have done for me in not changing your course towards the cross. Help me to live with grateful intentionality and an awareness of my final hour as I remember that the joy you have given me now is only a foretaste of what is still on the way.

"The joy of joys will be the delight of Christ in His perfectly gathered church. There is joy in heaven in the presence of the angels of God over one sinner that repents; but when all these repenting sinners are gathered into one perfected body, and married to the Lamb, what will be the infinite

gladness? Heaven is always heaven, and unspeakably full of blessedness—but even heaven has its holidays, even bliss has its overflowing; and on that day, when the springtide of the infinite ocean of joy shall have come, what a measureless flood of delight shall overflow the souls of all glorified spirits as they perceive that the consummation of love's great design is come—'The marriage of the Lamb is come, and His wife has made herself ready'. We do not know yet, beloved, of what happiness we are capable."

Charles Spurgeon, "The Marriage of the Lamb", Sermon #2096

CHAPTER 4

"Destroy this temple, and I will raise it up"

READ JOHN 2:18-22

*D*o you remember where you were on 31st December 2019? I know, I know—that feels like several lifetimes ago. We all had 99 problems, but a pandemic wasn't one of them. Looking optimistically ahead into the year 2020, there was the heightened sense of excitement that came with a new decade. Church leaders were breathless with anticipation at weaving the phrase "20/20 vision" into the first few weeks of the new year (probably).

But then Covid-19 happened. And all those hope-filled plans we all had for the coming year looked very, very different.

Frequently, the words that Jesus spoke with foresight were only understood by his disciples with hindsight. After Jesus had made a whip and cleansed the temple, the Jews asked him for a sign that would confirm the authority with which he had acted. His answer was prophetic yet cryptic: *"Destroy this temple, and in three days I will raise it up"* (John 2:19). We can forgive his hearers for missing his meaning, interpreting him literally rather than prophetically. He was, after all, *literally* standing in the temple. Again, what Jesus spoke with foresight about his own resurrection from death, the disciples only understood in hindsight. The temple he spoke of was not the building but his body.

Do you see the beauty and depth of what Jesus' words here mean for you and me today? The temple was marked out as the earthly container of God's glory, where the high priest would enter once a year into the very presence of God, where sacrifices for sin were offered up and forgiveness was poured down. Here, it is being identified with the human body of Jesus.

Little did the residents of Jerusalem know what was coming their way. Just a handful of decades later in AD 70, this same temple would be completely obliterated when the Roman army laid siege to their city. Not one stone would be left upon another, fulfilling another of Jesus' prophecies (Matthew 24:1-2). In the same way, we don't know what the path ahead is going to look like. Like a near-sighted driver navigating the road at nighttime, our foresight is dim and unreliable. We can barely make out what is coming our way.

But consider how frequently in your life so far that hindsight has given you insight into God's work in your own life. As with the disciples, looking back often has a way of providing us with a little more perspective. How much more so will everything that confuses and troubles us be made clear one day when we look back at our earthly lives from the standpoint of eternal life!

Yet in the meantime, our limited eyes and restless hearts can find rest in the hope that Jesus knows the end from the beginning. He is the Alpha and the Omega. Just as on that day in the temple, Jesus not only knows what is coming our way; he is sovereign over it. His purposes will be accomplished through it. I like how the New Living Translation paraphrases Paul's words in Romans 11:36: "For everything comes from him and exists by his power and is intended for his glory".

Upon the death and resurrection of Jesus, no longer would God's people need to come to a place to offer sacrifices for the forgiveness of sin. Now we can come to a person, Jesus, who has offered himself as the perfect sacrifice once and for all. And because of this, "we have confidence to enter the holy places by the blood of Jesus, by the new and living way that he opened for us through the curtain, that is, through his flesh" (Hebrews 10:19-20).

Jesus is the greater temple, in whom we have both forgiveness from God and access to God. As New Testament theologian Frederick Bruner writes, "The risen-crucified Messiah, Jesus, is the everywhere-available Presence and Temple of God".[6]

Jesus commands our future. He is the temple that could never be destroyed, and he is ever near to his people. His presence is the source of our confidence. His resurrection life will one day be ours in all its fullness. We can journey forward into what is unknown to us, assured that all is known by him.

REFLECT
If Jesus is the "everywhere-available Presence and Temple of God," how does that change the way you face the uncertainties you're dealing with this week?

"Only God knows the future. All things are present to him; there is no past and no future to his all-seeing eyes. He dwells in the present tense evermore as the great I AM. He knows what will be on the morrow, and he alone knows. The whole course of the universe lies before him, like an open map. Men do not know what a day

---

6 Frederick Dale Bruner, *The Gospel of John: A Commentary* (Eerdmans, 2012), p 147.

may bring forth, but Jehovah knows the end from the beginning. There are two great certainties about things that shall come to pass—one is that God knows, and the other is that we do not know."

Charles Spurgeon, "God's Will about the Future", Sermon #2242

CHAPTER 5

"You must be born again"

READ JOHN 3:1-8

When you think about it, your birthday is kind of weird. Each year, you have an entire day dedicated to being celebrated, sung to, stuffed with cake, and congratulated by everyone around you, for something that you contributed absolutely nothing to. You got born. Your contribution to the day of your birth, was, well, not exactly something you can boast in. If you don't believe me, just ask your mother.

No one wills themself into existence. We are *given* existence. If physical life is something that comes from outside of us, how much more so is spiritual life?

Nicodemus is a good man. He loves God, he loves the Scriptures, he is a devoted theologian, he is moral and upright, and he is a respected leader in Israel. And Jesus basically says to him, *It's not enough*.

The one thing Nicodemus needs is the one thing he cannot produce from within himself. He needs to be born *again*.

George Whitefield, the famous 17th-century evangelist and preacher, was said to have preached on the subject of "You must be born again" an estimated 3,000 times through the course of his life. For perspective, that's the equivalent of preaching the same text once a week for 57 years—a number made even more remarkable by the fact that Whitefield died at the age of 55. It's said that when someone once asked him, "Why, Mr Whitefield, do you so often preach on 'You must be born again?'" he replied, "Because… *you must* be born again!"

No one enters life with God by resolving to do better, turning over a new leaf, and trying their hardest.

The message of salvation is that God comes to *us*. The message of undeserved grace is that God moves toward *us*. Apart from his gracious initiative, we are, in the words of the apostle Paul, "dead in … sins … sons of disobedience … by nature children of wrath" (Ephesians 2:1-3). The miracle is in the next verse: "But God, being rich in mercy, because of the great love with which he loved us, even when we were dead in our trespasses, made us alive together with Christ—by grace you have been saved" (v 4-5). If salvation is by grace alone, then being a Christian is not merely the result of a good decision you made once; it's a miracle.

And just as with your birthday, there is nothing for you to boast in. But there are ten thousand upon ten thousand reasons for you to rejoice in the gift you've been given. In his best-selling book, *The Ragamuffin Gospel*, Brennan Manning describes the miracle of conversion like this:

> *"Over a hundred years ago in the Deep South, a phrase so common in our Christian culture today, born again, was seldom or never used. Rather, the phrase used to describe the breakthrough into a personal relationship with Jesus Christ was, 'I was seized by the power of a great affection.' These words describe both the initiative of God and the explosion within the heart when Jesus … becomes real, alive, and Lord of one's life."* [7]

---

7 Brennan Manning, *The Ragamuffin Gospel: Good News for the Bedraggled, Beat-Up, and Burnt Out* (Multnomah Books, 2005), p 195.

When Jesus said, "Unless one is born of water and the Spirit, he cannot enter the kingdom of God" (John 3:5), he probably had in mind the promise given through Ezekiel: "I will sprinkle clean water on you, and you shall be clean from all your uncleannesses ... I will give you a new heart, and a new spirit I will put within you" (Ezekiel 36:25-26). God does all the giving in salvation; all we do is receive. Jesus wants Nicodemus to be convinced that, as with Nicodemus' own birth, this new birth is something that comes from outside of himself. Why? So that Nicodemus would set his eyes and hope beyond himself rather than in himself.

Remember today that your Christian faith is a miracle. You are standing in the midst of a miracle, and so your faith was supernatural in its origin, is supernatural in its outworking, and will be supernatural in its outcome. Salvation is "the initiative of God" that pursues us and an "explosion within the heart" that renews us. So sing gladly the lines of the old hymn: "What can wash away my sin? Nothing but the blood of Jesus!" Stare amazed at the love of God, who "saved us, not because of works done by us in righteousness, but according to his own mercy, by the washing of regeneration and renewal of the Holy Spirit, whom he poured out on us richly through Jesus Christ our Saviour" (Titus 3:5-6).

PRAY
Lord, if you didn't first love me, I would have never loved you. Thank you for taking the initiative to pursue me. Let me live out of the joy of my salvation today.

"Our first birth makes us sons of Adam; our second birth makes us sons of God. Born of the flesh, we inherit

corruption—we must be born of the Spirit to inherit incorruption. We come into this world heirs of sorrow because we are sons of the fallen man. Our new life comes into the new world an heir of glory, because it is descended from the second man, the Lord from heaven."

Charles Spurgeon, "Every Man's Necessity", Sermon #1455

CHAPTER 6

"So must the Son of Man be lifted up"

READ JOHN 3:14-15

*H*ave you ever been out for a hike and taken a wrong turn? What about a wrong turn that added an extra 40 years to your trip? Still in conversation with Nicodemus, Jesus is recalling an experience that took place among God's people while walking through the wilderness to the promised land.

Faced with a distance that should have taken them less than two weeks on foot, they instead opted for the worst detour in the history of foot-travel, adding 40 years to their journey. The wrong turn wasn't external, however. It was internal.

A series of internal exchanges crept into their hearts. Faith in God's promised future was replaced with fear of the obstacles along the way. Gradually, trust was traded in for impatience, and impatience soon led to idolatry. The jubilant song of deliverance sung on the shores of the Red Sea had dissipated into a melancholic grumble of unbelief. Here's where Numbers 21 picks up the story:

> *"Then the LORD sent fiery serpents among the people, and they bit the people, so that many people of Israel died. And the people came to Moses and said, 'We have sinned, for*

*we have spoken against the LORD and against you. Pray
to the LORD, that he take away the serpents from us.' So
Moses prayed for the people. And the LORD said to Moses,
'Make a fiery serpent and set it on a pole, and everyone
who is bitten, when he sees it, shall live.' So Moses made
a bronze serpent and set it on a pole. And if a serpent bit
anyone, he would look at the bronze serpent and live."*
(Numbers 21:6-9)

Unbelief and serpents seem to be constantly linked in
Scripture, from the satanic whisper that led to the fall in
Genesis 3 to the narrative here in Numbers 21, to the imagery
of the Psalms and the prophets (Psalm 58:4-5; Jeremiah 8:17),
all the way to the rebuke of Jesus used for unbelieving religious
leaders ("You serpents, you brood of vipers..." Matthew
23:33). Unbelief happens when we start lifting up the wrong
thing. Instead of seeing God as he is—faithful to his promises,
sovereign in his authority and good in all his ways—we look
away to something else to give us fullness of life.

Jesus takes this incident in Numbers and uses it to prophesy
about what will happen to him on the cross. The remedy for sin's
fatal bite is simple yet profound. Like the bronze serpent of Moses,
Jesus will be lifted up on the cross. And whoever looks to him,
whoever "believes in him, [will] have eternal life" (John 3:15).

Is there anything more worthy of your gaze than Jesus?

Is there anything competing with him for the attention of
your eyes right now?

Is there anything that troubles your heart right now that
you are lifting up higher than him?

Jesus says, *Look to me and you shall live. I'm the one you're
looking for, today and every day that follows.*

PRAY

Lord, I do believe. But help my unbelief. Let nothing be
higher in my heart, my mind or my life than you.

"I sometimes think I might have been in darkness and despair until now, had it not been for the goodness of God in sending a snowstorm one Sunday morning while I was going to a certain place of worship.

"The minister did not come that morning; he was snowed in, I suppose. At last, a very thin-looking man, a shoemaker or a tailor or something of that sort, went up into the pulpit to preach. Now, it is well that preachers should be instructed; but this man was really stupid. He was obliged to stick to his text for the simple reason that he had little else to say ...

"Then, lifting up his hands, he shouted ... 'Young man, look to Jesus Christ. Look! Look! Look! You have nothin' to do but to look and live.' I saw at once the way of salvation. I know not what else he said—I did not take much notice of it—I was so possessed with that one thought. Like as when the brazen serpent was lifted up, the people only looked and were healed, so it was with me. I had been waiting to do fifty things, but when I heard that word, 'Look!' what a charming word it seemed to me! Oh! I looked until I could almost have looked my eyes away. There and then the cloud was gone, the darkness had rolled away, and that moment I saw the sun; and I could have risen that instant, and sung with the most enthusiastic of them of the precious blood of Christ, and the simple faith which looks alone to Him. Oh, that somebody had told me this before, 'Trust Christ, and you shall be saved.'"

Charles Spurgeon, *C.H. Spurgeon's Autobiography* (Fleming H. Revell, 1900), p 106

CHAPTER 7

"The fields are white for harvest"

READ JOHN 4:31-38

*M*ost cultures have an expression or two that serve as warnings against haste and hurry.

"Good things come to those who wait."

"Rome wasn't built in a day."

"Slow and steady wins the race."

In Jewish culture at the time of Jesus, "There are yet four months, then comes the harvest" had a similar meaning. This saying drew on the cycle of sowing and reaping—familiar in that agrarian setting—to point out that a person shouldn't expect to harvest a field that they had only planted that morning. Miracles don't happen overnight, after all.

But while that is always true in an agricultural sense, it is not so in a missional sense. Jesus warns us from settling for an evangelistic mindset that has forgotten that when *he* is involved, miracles *can* happen overnight. While patience in God's mission is vital for long-haul faithfulness, the harvest isn't only some time off in the future. There are people whom God intends to draw to himself—with saving, reviving impact—each and every day. Missionally speaking, patience in God's timing and trust in his sovereignty must never be separated from urgency in our present work. We must learn to believe with Paul that "indeed, the 'right time' is now. Today is the day of salvation" (2 Corinthians 6:2, NLT).

> *"Look, I tell you, lift up your eyes, and see that the fields are white for harvest." (John 4:35)*

Returning from town with lunch for Jesus, the disciples were shocked to find him engrossed in deep conversation with not merely a woman (which would probably raise some eyebrows), but a woman from a people group who were the declared enemy of their own: a *Samaritan*. Jesus had just prophetically revealed to her the depths of her own heart. But more than that, he had revealed to her the depths of his own heart: that he was the answer to her longings—he was the living water that could quench her thirst—because he was the promised Messiah (v 26). And at this revelation, her heart came alive with the joy of saving faith. It was the kind of joy that no matter how hard you try, you just cannot keep to yourself. The kind of joy that forces itself out of the mouth and into the ears of anyone who will listen. The kind of joy that goes hurrying into town with an invitation: *Come and see for yourself!*

And apparently, this evangelistic interaction had had a nourishing effect on Jesus himself! No longer hungry and fatigued by his journey, Jesus has been revitalised. He says to his disciples, "I have food to eat that you do not know about … My food is to do the will of him who sent me" (v 32, 34). He wants them to see something that he has, which they don't. He wants them to be aware of the satisfaction that comes by him living in congruence with his identity, as one who is "sent". He wants them to understand that the Father has woven our joy into his mission. And when God's mission becomes the lens through which we see our day—including those parts of our day that often seem like interruptions to our plans—there is a nourishing impact on our lives.

Because, after all, what is a sandwich compared to a soul?

God has woven *your* joy into *his* mission. Patience is most certainly a virtue in this great endeavour. Impassivity, however, is not. What if the boredom that you and I sometimes feel in our Christianity is actually God's alarm clock ringing in our hearts, alerting us to the absence of God's mission? Have we started to live as if God has saved us but doesn't intend to include us in the joyful work of anyone else's salvation story? Have we become discouraged along the way and stopped participating at a personal level in the Great Commission?

"Look, I tell you, lift up your eyes, and see that the fields are white for harvest." (v 35)

Let's open our eyes to the people God brings across our path this week, and follow Jesus into the Father's work that he has set before us. Will you make the following prayer your own today?

PRAY

Lord, help me to see the fields that are white for harvest around me. Give me an urgency in your mission, even as you give me trust in your sovereign timing. Help me to really believe that you intend to include me, and work through me, in the joy of drawing people to yourself.

"Some of you good people, who do nothing except go to public meetings, the Bible readings, and prophetic conferences, and other forms of spiritual dissipation, would be a good deal better Christians if you would look after the poor and needy around you. If you would just tuck up your

sleeves for work, and go and tell the Gospel to dying men, you would find your spiritual health mightily restored, for very much of the sickness of Christians comes through their having nothing to do. All feeding and no working makes men spiritual dyspeptics [suffering from indigestion] ... Do but win souls, beloved, through the power of the Holy Spirit, and you shall find it to be a perennial spring of joy in your own souls."

Charles Spurgeon, "A Golden Sentence", Sermon #3135

CHAPTER 8

"The Scriptures bear witness about me"

READ JOHN 5:39-40

*T*magine you are in a situation where a tornado or hurricane is bearing down on you. Lightning flashes all around. Thunder rumbles. Wind whips about you with what feels like malevolent intent. And there ahead of you is a door marked "Emergency Shelter". On the other side of it lies safety and life.

As you approach it, however, you notice a group gathered around it. They too sense the storm bearing down on them. But instead of entering in, they have struck up a conversation outside the door, about the door itself. Some are admiring it. Others are inspecting it, discussing the merits of the door for withstanding storms. But none have entered through it. They have completely missed the point of it.

Reading the Bible in a way that doesn't move us towards Jesus in worship and trust and hope is exactly the same. The Bible is not a destination in and of itself but a doorway into the life-renewing truth of who God is for us in Jesus Christ.

Jesus, here, was addressing a group of religious leaders who were very serious about the Old Testament Scriptures. They read them, searched them, memorised them and recited them. But they had missed the point of them.

The entire point of the entire Bible is Jesus.

While the Bible has instructions, it is not primarily a book of instruction.

While the Bible gives guidance, it is not primarily a manual for living well.

While the Bible tells many stories, they are far more than mere tales of heroic examples.

Jesus says of the Scriptures, *"They ... bear witness about me"* (John 5:39).

The story told a thousand different ways across the Old Testament is that, though we were made with dignity in the image of God himself (Genesis 1 – 2), every single one of us from Genesis 3 onward has rebelled against God and gone our own way. From Adam and Eve to Moses and the Israelites, to you and me in this present day and everyone in between—all have sinned and fallen tragically short of the glory for which God created us (Romans 3:23). Left to ourselves and our own ways, humanity is totally, collectively and hopelessly lost.

But that's only half the story of the Old Testament. The other half was the promise that God would send a Saviour. And in this way, the Old Testament prophesied, anticipated and pointed to what the New Testament reveals: God has fulfilled his every promise—in Jesus. The point of the Scriptures is not a "what" but a "who". To miss him is to miss everything.

> *"You search the Scriptures because you think that in them you have eternal life; and it is they that bear witness about me." (John 5:39)*

The problem was not in the commitment of these religious leaders to searching the Scriptures. We should indeed see ourselves as treasure hunters in the pages of God's word, convinced that every tunnel and crevice of Scripture is loaded with gold. As the psalmist declares, *"I rejoice at your word like one who finds great spoil"* (Psalm 119:162). The problem was they had focused on the wrong object in their search. These religious leaders were convinced that eternal life was found in their reverence for Scripture itself. Like a group of self-professed experts admiring a door to a shelter in the midst of a hurricane instead of entering through it, these religious leaders had missed the purpose of the Scriptures because they had missed the person about whom the Scriptures testified. And that person—Life himself—was staring them in the face.

How would your approach to Bible-reading change if each time you saw that precious book sitting there on your kitchen table or by your bed or on your desk, you saw not merely a destination (to which, you know, you really should pay a visit) but a daily doorway into life?

Every page bears witness about him.

Every story of imperfect people points to the great story of a perfect Saviour.

Every longing it evokes for a better future—for life as it is meant to be, for a day when sin is obliterated and glory is permanentized in your own life for ever—is met in him.

So as you open your Bible, remember not just to come to it. Come through it, to Jesus.

PRAY
Jesus, help me not only to read my Bible but to meet with you through my Bible. I do want to know more information *about* you. But even more than that, I want to *know* you.

"O living Christ, make this a living Word to me. Your Word is life, but not without the Holy Spirit. I may know this

*book of yours from beginning to end and repeat it all from
Genesis to Revelation, and yet it may be a dead book to
me and I may be a dead soul. But Lord, be present here;
then will I look up from the book to the Lord, from the
precept to Him who fulfilled it, from the law to Him who
honoured it, from the threatening to Him who has borne
it for me, and from the promise to Him in whom it is 'Yes
and amen.' Ah, then we shall read the book so differently.
He is here with me in this chamber of mine—I must not
trifle. He leans over me. He puts His finger along the
lines. I can see His pierced hand. I will read it as in His
Presence. I will read it knowing that He is the substance
of it, that He is the proof of this book as well as the writer
of it—the sum of this Scripture as well as the author of it.
That is the way for true students to become wise!"*

Charles Spurgeon, "How to Read the Bible", Sermon #1503

CHAPTER 9

"It is I; do not be afraid"

READ JOHN 6:16-21

*A*fter miraculously feeding a crowd of 5,000 plus with the bread and fish from a young boy's lunchbox, Jesus withdrew to be alone and sent the disciples across the sea ahead of him (John 6:15-17; Matthew 14:22-23). During the crossing, the wind whipped the sea into a frenzy, and the disciples were forced to row against the wind, until the figure of Jesus suddenly appeared to them like an apparition off in the distance, walking on top of the waves. Understandably, they became even more frightened.

Now, take a moment and try to put yourself in the boat with these disciples. John says they had rowed "about three or four miles" into a strong headwind before the figure of Jesus appeared, walking across the water (v 19). In Matthew's account, his appearance was in "the fourth watch of the night" (Matthew 14:25), which means sometime between 3 a.m. and 6 a.m. In other words, these men had been rowing into the wind, through dark and menacing waters, for roughly six to eight hours. This wasn't a few minutes of rowing through circumstances beyond their control. Not an hour or so. But nearly an entire night of trauma that had no discernible end in sight. It is not hard to imagine the disciples wondering, *Has Jesus forgotten us?*

And then in his own time, Jesus appears. Never once in his earthly life do we find Jesus in a hurry, and that is no less true here. In fact, John's recording of this miraculous moment paints Jesus with a surprising casualness. He is not panicked; he is *walking*. In the midst of nature's fury, he strolls with supernatural calm. Is it any wonder that the disciples were terrified that they were seeing a ghost (Matthew 14:26)?

It is here that Jesus announces himself with three simple words: *"It is I"*. And in his presence, their fears are exchanged for gladness. Interestingly, the whole encounter carries prophetic echoes from God's promise to his people through the prophet Isaiah. Look at these lines from within the first five verses of Isaiah 43:

> *"**Do not fear**, for I have redeemed you ...*
> *When you pass through the **waters, I will** be with you ...*
> *For **I am** the **LORD** your God,*
> *the Holy One of Israel, and your Saviour ...*
> ***Do not fear, for I am with you.***"
>
> *(v 1-5, CSB, emphasis mine)*

How would your life change if you remembered, and kept on remembering, that no matter what is happening around you, Jesus has not abandoned you? Martyn Lloyd-Jones has given one of my favourite definitions of what it looks like to trust in Jesus in the gritty moments of life: "Faith is the refusal to panic".[8]

After all, Jesus never promised us easy sailing. Just the opposite: "In the world you will have tribulation. But take heart; I have overcome the world" (John 16:33). In other words, if Jesus really is with us—truly, fully, inseparably and eternally with us—then for the rest of our lives, you and I will never have a single good reason to panic.

---

8 D. Martyn Lloyd-Jones, *Spiritual Depression: Its Causes and Cure* (Eerdmans: 1965), p.143.

Trouble is going to come. When it does, where will you fix your gaze?

Fix your eyes on the storms around you and your heart will be battered by despair. Fix your eyes on the resources within you and your hope will extend only as far as your creaturely limitations. Fix your eyes instead upon Jesus and you will discover sufficient grace woven into every present and future trouble.

He commands your fearlessness by announcing his presence: *"It is I; do not be afraid"*. There is no storm in your future that he will abandon you to face alone. There is no night so dark or wind so strong or wave so high that it will separate you from the ever-present and invincible nearness of Jesus.

How could it be otherwise? The one who called the elements of the physical universe into being rules them still. Jesus walked on top of the waves because even the waters recognised their rightful place under the feet of their Maker.

REFLECT

Where in your life do you need to draw strength from these words of your Saviour? *"It is I; do not be afraid."*

"It is Jesus who walks the water of your trouble and comes to you—Jesus the Son of God, the Alpha and the Omega, the Head over all things to His church—the All in all of all His people … The comfort of the Lord's people lies in the person and character of Jesus. Here is their solace: 'IT IS I'.

"But what a big 'I' it is. Compound in one all that is conceivable of goodness, and mercy, and grace, and faithfulness, and love—add perfect humanity, and infinite Godhead, and all the sovereign rights, powers, and

possessions of the Highest—and these are all contained in the one little letter 'I' when Jesus says, 'It is I; be not afraid'."

Charles Spurgeon, "Good Cheer from Christ's Real Presence", Sermon #3128

CHAPTER 10

"Whoever comes to me,
I will never cast out"

READ JOHN 6:37-39

One of the most astounding things about Jesus is how he exposes our preconceptions of what salvation requires, along with our misconceptions about God's heart toward us. In this passage, Jesus presents two important impossibilities when it comes to God's saving grace in someone's life.

Impossibility #1: That God would draw a person to Jesus and that they would *not* come to him. Jesus says, *"All* that the Father gives me *will* come to me" (John 6:37, my emphasis). In other words, if God sets his saving love upon a person, they shall, without exception, respond by coming to Jesus and trusting in him. He does this not by coercion or force but by melting their resistance with the blazing tenderness of sovereign grace.

Impossibility #2: That God would draw a person to Jesus, only to lose them at some later point in time. Jesus says, "Whoever comes to me I will *never* cast out ... This is the will of him who sent me, that I should lose *nothing* of all that he has given me" (v 37, 39, my emphasis). Our perseverance in Christ is because of God's perseverance with us. When God begins a good work in us, he is irreversibly committed to the completion of that work (Philippians 1:6).

So ask yourself: do I *really* believe this? For it is during our dark days, when we have wandered off into sin again or the self-loathing that follows it, that the impossibilities of grace become beaming rays of hope that draw us back to God. Knowing and believing that God's grace is even wider and deeper and longer and higher and better than we think does not cheapen grace. On the contrary, it is what gets our eyes off ourselves and catalyses our repentance.

Like a bucket of cold water to the face, the impossibilities of grace interrupt us. We are like the prodigal son rehearsing his "sorry" speech, who then looks up to the sight of his aged father running at breakneck speed towards with him wet cheeks and open arms, at which point our small thoughts of God's generosity are confronted by the impossibilities of grace. They sensitise us to how scandalously lovely grace really is.

"Whoever comes to me I will never cast out." (John 6:37)

It is so simple. Yet perhaps that's what makes us suspicious. The simplicity *is* the difficulty. It strikes us as too good to be true. So we complicate things with a thousand qualifications, conditions and footnotes that dilute the potency of his promise.

"Whoever comes to me I will never cast out."

Let every reason that might delay your coming to Jesus be broken on the anvil of that word "never." He will *never* turn you away or cast you out. "But what if I haven't repented thoroughly enough. Will he refuse me?" *Never.* "What if it's the ten millionth time. Will he throw in the towel on me?" *Never.* Far from inviting us to an audition where he will choose the high-achievers and the have-it-all-togethers who can produce the moral equivalent of an Olympic floor-gymnastics routine, all that Jesus requires of you is that you come to him. Now. Tomorrow. For ever. And he will never tire of receiving you. He is more than fine with high-maintenance people who are honest enough about their neediness to keep bringing it to him.

If Jesus makes such a promise towards you—despite the fickleness of your faith towards him—why would you *not* come to him?

"Whoever comes to me I will never cast out."

That's Christianity. Day in and day out, coming to Jesus. Walking with Jesus. Resting in Jesus. And—when we wander and come to our senses—returning to Jesus. Not because we think so lowly of his commands but because we are so highly convinced of the truth of his promises. In his book *Gentle and Lowly*, author Dane Ortlund concludes:

"The Christian life boils down to two steps:
1. Go to Jesus.
2. See [step] #1." [9]

How might you step out into each day if you really believed that this was the heart of Jesus towards you? That God is more committed to the saving work he began in you than you ever will be? *"Whoever comes to me I will never cast out."* On the last day, no one will accuse Jesus of failing to finish his saving work in the lives of any of his beloved. Everyone who will have come to him—without exception—will be raised up with him in resurrection glory. Let the glory of such a promise overshadow your every anxiety and doubt.

Go to him. He will never *not* receive you.

---

9 Dane Ortlund, *Gentle and Lowly: The Heart of Christ for Sinners and Sufferers* (Crossway, 2020), p 216.

PRAY

Jesus, forgive me for having small views of your grace. You are a better Saviour than I will ever be able to imagine. The work you have begun in my life is a work you intend to complete. When my faith is weak, your grip is not. Help me to remember that.

*"But let me also ask you, suppose that you came to Jesus and He cast you out, **with what hands could He do it?** 'With His own hands,' you answer. What! Christ coming forward to cast out a sinner who has come to Him? I ask again, with what hands could He do it? Would He do it with those pierced hands, that still bear the marks of the nails? The Crucified rejecting a sinner? Ah! No, He has no hand with which to do such a cruel work as that, for He has given both His hands to be nailed to the tree for guilty men. He has neither hand, nor foot, nor heart with which to reject sinners, for all these have been pierced in His death for them; therefore He cannot cast them out if they come to Him."*

Charles Spurgeon, "All Comers to Christ Welcomed", Sermon #2349

CHAPTER 11

"I am the living bread that came down from heaven"

READ JOHN 6:47-51

I love bread. Actually, I can't even begin to tell you how much I love bread. Perhaps the fact that I am sitting here right now on month 4 of the very breadless Keto diet wondering if the new creation will include a reconciliation between humanity and carbs is a decent indicator that I might love bread a little too much.

The previous day, Jesus had satisfied the physical hunger of thousands of people, through the miracle with two fish and five loaves of bread. The masses found him the following day and demanded that he repeat the miracle, as a guise for getting more free food. Jesus had become a means to an end—namely, filling their stomachs. They wanted the gifts but the Giver not so much.

So they came reminding Jesus of how God provided their ancestors with miraculous bread in the wilderness at the beginning of each day; it was called "manna"—a Hebrew word meaning "What is it?" Each morning, to keep them from starving on their journey from Egypt to the promised land, God covered the ground with it. Exodus 16:14-15 records their wonder at the daily miracle the first time it happened:

"And when the dew had gone up, there was on the face of the wilderness a fine, flake-like thing, fine as frost on the ground. When the people of Israel saw it, they said to one another, 'What is it?' For they did not know what it was. And Moses said to them, 'It is the bread that the LORD has given you to eat.'"

But here was the catch: manna only lasted for a day. If you tried to store up enough to last for the rest of the week, it would spoil and rot. It was momentary satisfaction. And ultimately, each person who ate it and lived through another day eventually died (John 6:49). Manna satisfied hunger but only for a day.

And so it is with every created thing. In the same way that only physical food can satisfy physical hunger, only spiritual food can satisfy spiritual hunger. Not even 24 hours earlier, the crowds had experienced a miracle. And yet already the miracle had become manna to them. It was no longer enough. Are we that different? Don't we find ourselves trying to scratch an eternal itch with temporary and material things?

It is in this context that Jesus looks at these people and says the first of his seven famous "I am" sayings in John's Gospel: *"I am the bread of life ... I am the living bread that came down from heaven. If anyone eats of this bread, he will live for ever"* (v 48, 51). Jesus is confronting the pragmatist in all of us that tends to focus only on that which is temporary, while forgetting that which will last for ever. He is exposing the bankruptcy of a definition of life that is limited to the material world. The Puritan pastor Thomas Brooks put it like this: "A man may have enough of the world to sink him, but he can never have enough to satisfy him." This is why Jesus would later ask a different group of people, "What does it profit a man to gain the whole world and forfeit his soul?" (Mark 8:36).

So where will you look for satisfaction and strength today?

Despite the countless good gifts God has given us in the created world, none of them will adequately deal with the deeper hunger we all have for a meaningful, well-nourished life. How could they? They were never designed to. No matter how much you accumulate or achieve or experience, it will never be enough to satisfy.

We could search the entire world and experience everything it offers ten thousand times over. And we'd end up concluding with Solomon (who pretty much tried that) that "All is vanity. What does man gain by all the toil at which he toils under the sun?" (Ecclesiastes 1:2-3).

Or we could come to the Saviour.

Jesus is both the daily bread that strengthens us for the moment and the eternal bread that satisfies his people for ever. When was the last time you slowed down enough to gaze at the glory of God in who Jesus Christ is and let your heart be satisfied by him? The meal you ate two months ago on a Wednesday is not sufficient for your present hunger. Come to him again today. Give yourself to him with honesty about your need and receive from him the life you most long to know.

PRAY
Lord, you have made me for yourself. And my heart is restless until it finds rest in you. (Augustine)

"Now, as a man who has feasted well, and is no more hungry, rises from the table satisfied, so we feel that in Jesus our entire nature has all that it needs! Christ is all, and we are filled in Him, complete in Him! This is to receive Christ! Beloved, if you want to have Christ altogether your own, you must receive Him by this process.

Merely to trust Him gives you Christ as food in your mouth; to contemplate, to meditate, to commune with Him is to understand Him, even as food is digested and is ours. Further prayer, and fellowship, and meditation assimilate Christ so that He becomes part and parcel of our very selves. Christ lives in us, and we in Him!"

Charles Spurgeon, "Soul-Satisfying Bread", Sermon #1112

CHAPTER 12

"Do you want to go away as well?"

READ JOHN 6:60-69

After claiming to the crowds, "I am the bread of life" (John 6:35), Jesus took his audacity even further. He told them that unless a person eats his flesh and drinks his blood, they cannot know eternal life (v 53-54). While many were undoubtedly confused by his words, Jesus was not calling his followers to a bizarre form of messianic cannibalism. The conversation around the table during the Last Supper would reveal that Jesus had had his death on the cross in mind (see Matthew 26:26-29).

But Jesus doesn't explain that here.

Amid the confusion, however, one thing was clear to everyone present: you could not half-follow Jesus. You could not half-trust Jesus. You could not half-love Jesus.

And many turned away.

What is most remarkable in this passage, however, is not that the crowds turned away. That's not surprising; crowds are notoriously fickle. What's remarkable is that John says that many of Jesus' *disciples* turned away. The eager ones. The previously committed ones. The men and women who were interested in a "moderate discipleship" of Jesus. Yet, as the renowned 20th-century author C.S. Lewis wrote, "Christianity, if false, is of no importance, and if true, of infinite importance. The only thing it cannot be is moderately important."[10]

And it is at this point that Jesus turns and looks at the Twelve and says, "Do you want to go away as well?" He was not asking for the sake of his own clarity about who would still follow him; he was asking for their sake. The question is less a question and more a gentle challenge.

To absolutely no one's surprise, Peter is the first to pipe up. Yet despite his deserved reputation for putting his foot in his own mouth, on this occasion Peter nails it. He responds to Jesus with a question that reveals the heart of a true disciple—a heart that has looked at Jesus, then looked at everything else the world offers in contrast, and seen that only one path leads to life as it is meant to be.

Peter replies, "Lord, to whom shall we go? You have the words of eternal life, and we have believed, and have come to know, that you are the Holy One of God" (John 6:68-69).

"You have the words of eternal life."

Peter understood that following Jesus would not be easy. But it would be true. And beautiful. And better. Sooner or later, every follower of Jesus must make peace with the reality that discipleship of Jesus comes with a cost. It requires trusting Jesus, even when it seems like it will cost us everything. But like Peter—and all who have had their hearts come alive through the explosive initiative of God's grace—we too can only reply, *"Lord, to whom shall we go?"*

I am reminded of the story behind the words that many of us have sung in various forms:

---

10 C.S. Lewis, *God in the Dock: Essays on Theology and Ethics* (Eerdmans, 1994), p 101.

I have decided to follow Jesus,
no turning back, no turning back.
The cross before me, the world behind me,
no turning back, no turning back.

It's said that in the later years of the 19th century and among great persecution, a Welsh missionary to the Assam region of India finally saw his first converts to Christianity. A husband and wife, along with their children, turned to Jesus and were baptised. Their village leaders, desiring to dissuade others from following them, arrested the family and demanded that they turn away from Jesus or they would forfeit their lives.

The husband responded, "I have decided to follow Jesus, and there's no turning back".

And they killed his children.

Again, he was commanded to renounce his Christianity. Yet he said to his persecutors, "Though no one joins me, still I will follow Jesus".

And they killed his wife.

With a final warning, they gave him one last chance to live. He replied, "The cross is before me, and the world is behind me. I won't turn back."

And he joined his family in martyrdom, rejected by this world but embraced by Jesus.

Disciples of Jesus have learned, and continue to relearn, that to possess the entire world apart from Jesus is the greatest poverty. Yet to have Jesus, without anything else, is to possess a richness that surpasses the combined wealth of the created universe.

REFLECT

Take a moment and consider the roads you might have gone down if not for Jesus. Who you would be if not for his grace?

"Now Christ seems to me to put this solemn, personal question to you, my dear brethren and sisters in Christ. Will you go away from Him after all that He has done for you? You believe that you have been called by His grace, for you have enjoyed the sweetness of His love, and you have been admitted into close personal fellowship with Him ... [If] you bear your willing witness that He is a gracious Lord and Master, and that He has been a precious Christ to you; indeed you say that He is your all in all, and that words fail you to tell all that you think of Him, then can you, will you go away from Him after all this?

"No, we must cling to Him whatever happens, for there is nothing or no one that can ever take His place."

Charles Spurgeon, "Clinging to Christ", Sermon #3210

CHAPTER 13

"If anyone thirsts, come to me and drink"

READ JOHN 7:37-39

*M*ost of us take water for granted. Theoretically we know that we need it to live. But having it so readily available to us in such an abundance of options (Sparkling? Still? Flavoured? Coconut? Gatorade? Aloe Vera?!), we don't really give it too much thought. None of us lay our head on our pillow at night and reflect back on our day thinking, "What an important drink of water that was for me at 1:14 p.m. I am so grateful!"

And while it is true that a drink of water is only a few steps away for most of us reading this book, in the context in which Jesus speaks these words—in Jerusalem, amid the arid desert that makes up much of the Middle East—people were all too aware that the presence of thirst combined with the absence of water meant only one thing: death. Biblically speaking, a thirsty person is a dying person. In this light, Jesus' words become not only weightier but incomparably more wonderful.

"If anyone thirsts, come to me and drink." (John 7:37)

Thirst is an inbuilt warning signal, alerting us to the presence of an absence. A lack. A desperate need, crying out for relief. Both physically and spiritually, dehydration that is left unchecked will kill us. And Jesus wants us to see that our spiritual thirst is satisfied in the provision that God alone gives.

In fact, the imagery of thirst, as it relates to human neediness, and water, as it relates to God's gracious provision for that need, flows throughout the Old Testament. In the psalms, David wrote, "As the deer pants for flowing streams, so pants my soul for you, O God" (Psalm 42:1). Isaiah referenced water frequently, giving both a promise and an invitation: "With joy you will draw water from the wells of salvation … Come, everyone who thirsts, come to the waters" (Isaiah 12:3; 55:1). God says through Jeremiah, "My people have committed two evils: they have forsaken me, the fountain of living waters, and hewed out cisterns for themselves, broken cisterns that can hold no water" (Jeremiah 2:13).

That last passage in Jeremiah is profound. It reminds us that everyone is looking for life, but there's only one "fountain of living waters". This is why the Early Church Father Augustine—after spending his life looking for love among the "broken cisterns" of fleeting pleasures—famously prayed, "You have made us for yourself, O Lord, and our heart is restless until it rests in you".

The invitation of Jesus offers more than just a cup that satisfies for a moment. He promises a spring of living water that will become a constant presence in our hearts for every thirst we will ever experience as he fills us with his Spirit. In other words, Jesus is not merely *sufficient* for your present temptations and restlessness. He is *overflowing* with the deeper kind of spiritual life and fulfilment that we most long to know. His invitation to a thirsty woman in John 4, who had been searching for satisfaction in all the wrong places, is the same invitation that he extends to you in this very moment:

Come to me and drink. Come to me, and live.

When Jesus made this invitation in John 7:37, it was the last day of an important annual feast known as the Festival of Shelters. During this celebration, God's people would build little shelters all over Jerusalem to remember their time of wandering in the wilderness and the way in which God had provided for them. Provision which, at key moments in their journey, included the miraculous supplying of water in the desert. Jesus was declaring, *I am that provision. I am the relief your thirst demands. I am the answer to your heart's every longing.*

He was promising to supply their deepest need.

He was reminding them that God alone is their Provider and that the Spirit is their Provision.

He wants them—and us—to become convinced that the remedy for our restlessness is not in an ideal circumstance or another new experience. The quenching of our thirst will not come through any personal achievement or career success. The satisfaction our hearts long for won't be found in trying harder, doing better, or being "true to ourselves". Our thirst alerts us to a need that is met in him. And only in him. Yet abundantly in him as he fills us with his Spirit.

So are you thirsty?

Are you looking elsewhere for something that Jesus alone can give?

Go to him again today in prayer. His invitation is wide open to you: *"If anyone thirsts, come to me and drink".*

PRAY

Lord, you are the satisfaction my heart most longs for. Quench my restless heart with living water. Shower the dry places of my life with your presence. Teach me not to go looking in deserts and broken cisterns for the life-renewing power that you alone can give.

"Whatsoever many things the soul thirsts for, Jesus will supply them all; our wonderful variety of wants is met by His wonderful variety of excellences. Here is a soul that wants peace—'this Man shall be the peace.' 'I am unhinged, I am almost driven to distraction, I am sorely troubled, so that I cannot sleep.' You shall have rest by coming to Jesus; 'He gives His beloved sleep.' 'But I am so guilty; I have sinned past all pardon; I blush to think how grievously I have trespassed.' You can have pardon for all your sins, though they are as glaring as scarlet, and though for number they are as many as the sands of the sea."

Charles Spurgeon, "The Preacher's Last Sermon for the Season", Sermon #1875

CHAPTER 14

"Neither do I condemn you"

READ JOHN 8:2-11

One of the most important questions that we will ever face is this: how will Jesus treat us when we *really* drop the ball? When we not only sin but "sin *big*". When we are caught red-handed. When that selfishness or pride or lust or anger or cowardice that has been hiding in the dark corners of our heart is brought into the light.

How will Jesus deal with you on *that* day?

While Jesus was in the middle of teaching a crowd of people outside of the temple, a woman who had been caught in the act of adultery was brought before him. Not only was she undeniably guilty but she was also now being publicly humiliated, knowing full well that she was on her way to be condemned and executed according to the Law of Moses.

She probably didn't wake up that morning intending that day to be the worst day of her life. None of us do that. Yet for her, today was *that* day.

And though her guilt was clear, something was clearly off. Why was only the woman brought to Jesus and not the man she was involved with? Why did the Pharisees—considered to be experts in Old Testament Scripture—only refer to the part of the law that condemned the woman but not the part that equally condemned the man (Leviticus 20:10)?

The whole scene reeked of hypocrisy, and Jesus could smell it. Those who were doing the accusing here didn't actually care about justice (evidenced by the absence of the man), and they didn't care about God's word (evidenced by their manipulation of Scripture). They cared only about undermining Jesus in order to exalt themselves. To them, this woman was nothing more than bait in an ethical trap. If Jesus condemned her, his reputation as a man of mercy would suffer. If he did not, his reputation as a man of holiness who upheld the Scriptures would suffer.

What does Jesus say to this woman's accusers on the worst day of her life?

He tells them to go ahead and stone her. But there's one small caveat: let the one who is without sin go first (John 8:7).

As the gravity of Jesus' words dawned on everyone present, the initial silence would have been deafening. One by one, her accusers realised that the first stone wouldn't be coming from their hands. Then, for a few holy minutes, the only sounds to be heard were those of rocks falling softly out of unclenched hands into the dirt and footsteps receding into the distance. Before long it was just the woman and Jesus. And here's how he responded:

> *"'Woman, where are they? Has no one condemned you?'*
> *She said, 'No one, Lord.' And Jesus said, 'Neither do I*
> *condemn you; go, and from now on sin no more.'"*
>
> *(John 8:10-11)*

You see, the only person in that crowd—and in the entire history of the world—qualified to throw the first stone was Jesus. And on the worst day of this woman's life, the one who exclusively possesses the right to condemn her forgave her. As Matt Carter writes, "Not only does he forgive her, but he also transforms her future. He doesn't give her a license to keep sinning. He gives her a reason to stop."[11]

That is how Jesus treats us when we "sin big". And that is what makes grace amazing: the verdict precedes the instruction. His undeserved acquittal of our sins not only comes before any action he calls us to; it empowers that very action. The order matters.

You are forgiven; now go and live like it.

You are accepted; now go and live like it.

You are loved; now go and live like it.

You are no longer condemned; now go and live like it.

Consider the cross that Jesus was moving toward throughout these final years of his life. There, he would bear the entirety of your condemnation. There, he would pay the price for your every sin in full. That means that if you belong to Jesus, then never again will you face the condemnation that you rightfully deserve. What powers God's plan of redemption forward in the lives of all his children is not karma but grace. Karma tells us that you get what you deserve. But the gospel of grace tells us that, in Jesus, we get what we don't deserve. Only the second is good news. And that's why no one ever wrote a song called, "Amazing Karma".

The motivation to change comes from believing that Jesus' verdict about you is so glorious and final, and that his grace toward you is so sufficient and permanent, that every part of your life is worthy of coming under his loving authority.

PRAY

Lord, I so often get it backwards. Help me to remember that your love is what empowers my repentance, not the other way around. I come to you today remembering that you have taken away all my condemnation, which means only you are worthy of all my obedience.

---

11 Matt Carter and Josh Wredberg, *Exalting Jesus in John* (Holman Reference, 2017), p 185.

"If you have ever been burdened with a sense of sin you will know the sweetness of the [promise]. You that are not sinners, you good respectable people who are sailing to heaven in your own ship, there is nothing in it for you. Gospel assurances are not for you; you would not prize them, and therefore you have neither part nor lot in them. For, Jesus Christ came not to call the righteous but sinners to repentance. But you that have been whipped of the devil and dragged at the heels of your sins, you that have been broken and crushed ... till you are ground fine under the hand of conviction, you are the people that will leap for joy as you hear the silver trumpet ring out the note of 'no condemnation'. Come, let us be glad. Let us rejoice together because there is now no condemnation to us."

Charles Spurgeon, "In Christ No Condemnation", Sermon #1917

CHAPTER 15

"I am the light of the world"

READ JOHN 8:12

*T*here were plenty of things that I loved about living in Seattle for a couple of years. Perfect summers. Gorgeously green landscapes, dotted with crystal-blue alpine lakes. Top Pot Doughnuts.

But one major drawback—particularly for a family of Australians—were the long grey stretches of sunless winters (fortunately, these usually didn't last any longer than ten months at a time). Navigating these seasons of prolonged sunlessness was hard. On one occasion, we went nearly two entire months without seeing the sun. It had been so long that when a ray of sunlight finally broke through the clouds, our 18-month-old son started playing with it, trying to grab hold of something that he probably thought he was encountering for the first time!

Light is vital. Light reveals the way forward. It comes as no surprise that the absence of sunlight has been linked with depression in some cases, as well as with a host of physical health conditions. Whether it's the flourishing of a plant or a person, light is vital for life.

And Jesus says that is what he is:

"I am the light of the world." (John 8:12)

He doesn't say that he is the light of one people group. Nor that he is one of many lights available to give direction to our lives. His claim is that he is *the* light of *the* world. Jesus is appropriating the rich Old Testament imagery of God being the light of his people. So David said, "The LORD is my light and salvation; whom shall I fear?" (Psalm 27:1); Isaiah declared, "The LORD shall be your everlasting light" (Isaiah 60:20); and Micah confessed, "When I sit in darkness, the LORD will be a light to me" (Micah 7:8). Jesus is claiming, *They're all talking about me.*

"I am the light of the world."

And his audacious claim is followed by an equally audacious promise: "Whoever follows me will not walk in darkness, but will have the light of life". What does Jesus mean by this? Clearly, he does not mean that his followers will never sin or suffer. If that were the mark of discipleship, none of us would be able to call ourselves followers of Jesus. Repenting of sin and enduring through suffering are both normal parts of the Christian life (1 John 1:8-10; Philippians 1:29).

No, what Jesus gives here is the despair-incinerating, confidence-renewing promise that everyone who follows him will never be abandoned by him. They will not be given completely over to darkness—they will not walk in the perpetual darkness that is reserved for those who reject God. Though they most certainly will experience dark nights of the soul and though dark clouds of suffering will sometimes obscure their view for a time, they will never walk in darkness. They will only ever walk *through* it.

This is how Jesus wants his followers to view their lives: through the lens of his light. Every atom of meaning and transcendence and beauty and goodness and hope exists only because he does. It's what C.S. Lewis meant when he wrote, "I believe in Christianity as I believe that the Sun has risen: not only because I see it, but because by it I see everything else".[12]

So when difficult days come for you, remember this: Jesus has not now abandoned and won't ever abandon you. The occurrence of such days does not mean that he has broken his promise to you. No, it is on such days that his promise becomes unspeakably precious, breaking through every storm cloud with invincible power as you remember that Jesus is "the light [that] shines in the darkness, and the darkness has not overcome it" (John 1:5). And it never will.

Not for Jesus. And not for you.

Where do you need to remember that today?

PRAY

Thank you, Lord, that no matter how dark this world gets or how difficult my circumstances become, nothing will ever extinguish your light. I confess that you are the light of the world, and the light of my world. Your light is the hope of my life. Your promises to me are the fuel for my following of you.

"Oh, [if you were] without Christ, my soul, what would you do in the world without Him, in the midst of its temptations and its cares? What would you do in the morning without Him, when you wake up and look forward to the day's battle? What would you do if He did not put His hand upon you, and say, 'Fear not, I am with you'? And what would you do at night, when you come home jaded and weary, if there were no prayer, no door of access between you and Christ? What would we do without Christ in our trials, our sicknesses? ... But, beloved, we need

---

12 C.S. Lewis, "Is Theology Poetry?" in *The Weight of Glory* (Colliers Books, 1980), p 92.

not suppose such a thing, for we know that our Redeemer lives, and we know that He never forsakes the work of His own hand! ... Of every day and every night, of every joy and every sorrow, the Lamb has been, until now, our light, and shall be till we die."

Charles Spurgeon, "The Lamb—The Light", Sermon #583

CHAPTER 16

"Before Abraham was, I am"

READ JOHN 8:52-59

$\mathcal{T}$he ancient Greek philosopher Heraclitus famously said, "The only constant in life is change". In many ways, the rate of change in our world has only accelerated over the past century. Through rapid advances in technology, we have more global mobility, more information at our fingertips, and more ways to connect to what is happening around the globe in real time than any generation before us. The pace at which society is changing—particularly in politically and culturally polarised Western contexts—can feel dizzying. We sense impermanence all around. Heraclitus' quip naturally resonates with us.

And yet, according to Jesus, Heraclitus was wrong.

In what is probably the clearest self-reference to his own deity, Jesus applies the never-wavering, perfect permanency of God to himself.

"Truly, truly, I say to you, before Abraham was, I am."
(John 8:58)

Jesus dropped this bomb at the end of a very long and very blunt conversation with a group of Jewish leaders. Did I say very blunt? I meant *extremely* blunt. Back in verse 44, Jesus had told them that the reason why they rejected him was because their father was the devil and they were self-deceived liars just like their spiritual dad—Satan. It's little wonder that this scene ends with rocks in their hands and murder in their hearts.

And here in verse 58, Jesus makes an identity claim so audacious that, if false, it is nothing less than the blasphemy of a megalomaniac. But if it's true, it is among the most important sentences in the world.

One of the most profound and revealing encounters with God recorded in the Bible is in Exodus 3. In the presence of a burning bush, and having received a promise of salvation, Moses asks God to tell him his name. But God doesn't respond with a name. He responds with a statement of his permanence. An eternal fact. The supreme truth upon which every other truth is dependent. God says to Moses, "I AM WHO I AM" (v 14). God is saying to Moses, *I have always been. And I will never not be. I am. And because I am, everything else is.* And here in John 8, this defining centre of existence—the unchanging constant that holds the universe together by the word of his power (Hebrews 1:3)—is standing right in front of his creatures.

"*I am.*"

Two little words that carry nuclear impact. Two little words that locate God as the ever-present centre of gravity around which every other reality orbits.

"*I am.*"

And Jesus takes these two explosive little words—the very words of God in Exodus 3 about his own unchanging permanence—and repeats what he had said centuries earlier to that other Jewish leader who had questions about his identity.

How can this be? Because the one who has not yet lived 50 years in the world, as his accusers point out, is the same one who pre-dates the oldest among them. And Moses. And Abraham. And the entire world. As Frederick Bruner writes, "Abraham was; Jesus is. Abraham was a man of God; Jesus is—God as man."[13]

> *"Truly, truly, I say to you, before Abraham was, I am."*
> *(John 8:58)*

In a world that changes like the sands of the desert, when do you need to remember that "Jesus Christ is the same yesterday and today and for ever" (Hebrews 13:8)? In times of constant uncertainty, when do you need to return to Jesus as the great and certain and enduring constant? He is the Rock, which time and storms will never erode. He is the King—"faithful and true" (Revelation 19:11)—whose promises and rule can be trusted. He is the Morning Star, who will never mislead any who look to him. He is the Eternal One. He is the Ancient of Days. He *is*.

PRAY

Jesus, you are my rock and sure foundation in this shifting world. All my hope is in your promises. All my days are in your hands. All that I am is only because you are. Thank you.

> *"If He be the same today as yesterday, my soul, set not your affections upon these changing things, but set your heart upon Him. O my heart, build not your house upon the sandy pillars of a world that soon must pass away, but build your hopes upon this rock, which, when the rain descends and floods shall come, shall stand immovably secure ... O*

---

13 Frederick Dale Bruner, *The Gospel of John: A Commentary* (Eerdmans, 2012), p 553.

my heart, I bid you now put your treasure where you can never lose it—put it in Christ. Put all your affections in His person, all your hope in His glory, all your trust in His efficacious blood, all your joy in His presence—and then you will have put yourself and put your all where you can never lose anything, because it is secure."

Charles Spurgeon, "The Immutability of Christ", Sermon #170

CHAPTER 17

"I am the good shepherd"

READ JOHN 10:11-15

*P*ride of lions. Pod of dolphins. Litter of bear cubs. Mob of kangaroos. There were so many potentially awesome possibilities. But throughout the Old and New Testaments, of all the animal options that the Scriptures could have used as a metaphor for God's people, God chose to go with sheep.

A flock of sheep. That's us, fellow-Christians. How... underwhelming.

Sheep aren't exactly known for being powerful or awe-inspiring. When we think of sheep, none of us really think of a creature likely to make it as the mascot of a professional sports team or onto a show of *Nature's Most Impressive Animals*. Sheep have no defence mechanisms. They are not known for their speed, agility, strength or brilliance. They are quite often stubborn, prone to wandering away, with almost no sense of direction. Which means that when they do wander off, they can't find their way back home.

Morally and spiritually speaking, that's us for sure.

Sheep are not impressive or self-sufficient creatures. Sheep need a shepherd.

But that's the point, isn't it?

The Bible isn't about how amazing you and I are. It's about

Jesus and how glorious and good and amazing he is. And twice in this passage Jesus says who he is and what he came to do.

"I am the good shepherd. The good shepherd lays down his life for the sheep." (John 10:11)

Consider the significance of Jesus being the "good shepherd" when it comes to your own life under his leadership. Here is why you can trust him with anything: the good shepherd is not a hired hand, and the difference between the two could not be starker.

Unlike the hired hand, the good shepherd knows each and every one of his sheep by name. And they respond to his voice. Unlike the hired hand, the good shepherd cares for his sheep. He does not abandon them in times of trouble. He defends them. He provides for them. He is near to them. It's what he loves to do. It's what he has always done.

Do you remember King David's most famous song—Psalm 23—where he described the Lord as a shepherd who renews him with green pastures, who leads him beside still waters and along paths of righteousness, and who is with him always, even through the darkest valleys? Jesus is saying here in John 10, *David was talking about me.* Jesus is the good shepherd who melts away our suspicions with the promise "I will never leave you nor forsake you" (Hebrews 13:5). And in response, "we can confidently say, 'The Lord is my helper; I will not fear; what can man do to me?'" (v 6).

And when we are tempted to wonder if God is holding out on us in some way, we only need remember that Jesus is the *good* shepherd, who cares for his sheep by laying down his own life for them. Countless sheep throughout the Old Testament were sacrificed at the temple for the sins of their shepherds. But here, at the turning point of history, the good shepherd shed his blood for the sheep once and for all. Before you had prayed one prayer, obeyed one command, or taken one step to follow him, Jesus, the great shepherd, laid down his life for you. One of the most marvellous gospel paradoxes is that the good shepherd is also the Lamb that was slain.

> *"I am the good shepherd. The good shepherd lays down his life for the sheep."*

Jesus is the good shepherd who knows you—the real you—yet he does not despise you.

Jesus is the good shepherd who is Lord of all, but not in a way that will crush you.

Jesus is the good shepherd who so loves you that he sacrificed himself for you.

Which means you don't have to be worry about being impressive, jostling to be accepted or hustling to be a "somebody". Just be impressed with Jesus. Hear his call and follow him wherever he leads you. He is the good shepherd. In light of that, what can't you entrust into his hands today?

PRAY

Personalise and pray Psalm 23: "Lord, you are my shepherd. I have everything I need. You make me lie down in green pastures. You lead me beside still waters. You restore my soul. You lead me on paths of righteousness for your name's sake. Even though I walk through the valley of the shadow of death, I will fear no evil, for you are with me; your rod and your staff, they comfort me. You prepare a table before me in the presence of my enemies; you anoint my head with oil; my cup overflows. Surely goodness and mercy shall follow me all the days of my life, and I shall dwell in the house of the Lord for ever."

"If Jesus is so pleased to be my Shepherd, let me be equally pleased to be His sheep, and let me avail myself of all the privileges that are wrapped up in His being my Shepherd, and in my being His sheep. I see that it will not worry Him for me to be His sheep. I see that my needs will cause Him no perplexity. I see that He will not be going out of His way to attend to my weakness and trouble. He delights to dwell on the fact: 'I am the good Shepherd'. He invites me, as it were, to come and bring my wants and woes to Him, look up to Him, and be fed by Him. Therefore I will do it."

Charles Spurgeon, "Our Own Dear Shepherd", Sermon #1877

CHAPTER 18

"My sheep
will never perish"

READ JOHN 10:27-30

*H*ere's a weird question for you: if you were to grade Jesus in his divine role of Saviour, would you be willing to flunk him? Probably not. What about giving a B+ though? Would you be willing to give Jesus a B+? Or anything less than perfect marks?

Ok, ok, I hear you. Grading Jesus might be ~~slightly~~ infinitely above your pay grade. We may as well ask an ant to evaluate the works of Mozart. But what if it were Jesus himself doing the grading? If Jesus—the sinless and perfect one—were to perform an honest self-assessment on his work as a Saviour, would his honesty force him to admit that he might at some time have dropped the ball on one of his people, or even that he had the potential to do so?

John 10:27-30 is one of those passages where Jesus makes sure that everyone understands the definiteness with which he saves his people. Here, anxious sinners and inconsistent disciples can come and drink from the waters of assurance. Look at each verse and press these words into your heart.

In verse 27, Jesus says that he knows his sheep and that his sheep know his voice, and the evidence of that is that they follow him. That isn't to say that they do not wander. Sheep do. But when Jesus calls, the deepest desire of their heart is to run toward their Shepherd.

Then in verse 28, Jesus reaffirms that he is the one who gives newness and fullness of life. And everyone who receives that life "will never perish, and no one will snatch them out of [his] hand." Take a moment and consider the weight of this. Has Jesus given you new life in him? Then you will never perish. It is impossible for him to lose you or for something to separate you from him.

In other words, when we wonder if Christians can lose their salvation, we are asking the wrong question. The right question, according to John 10:28, is: can Jesus lose a Christian? Can the "Lord Jesus, the great shepherd of the sheep" (Hebrews 13:20), lose a single member of his flock? Jesus answers our anxieties with a glorious certainty: his sheep will never perish. This is why Paul was convinced that nothing in all creation "will be able to separate us from the love of God in Christ Jesus our Lord" (Romans 8:39). No one will snatch Jesus' people out of his saving grip; no one will separate them from his love.

And then, just to make sure we are not still wondering, Jesus puts the final nail in the coffin of our doubts with John 10:29-30. The success of Jesus in accomplishing his mission is grounded in the eternal decree of the Father. For Jesus to fail as the Saviour, the triune God would have to fail at being God.

How can this be? Because, Jesus declares, *"I and the Father are one"*. Consider the impact of these words. To the degree that Jesus is secure in the grip of the Father, every single Christian is secure in the grip of the Son. The only way that Christ's sheep will ever perish is if Christ himself were to perish with them. Jesus will be removed from his throne in heaven before any of his children are removed from his saving embrace.

So inhale who Jesus really is for you and exhale every fear of the future that troubles you. Your security is not in the determination with which you hold on to Jesus but in the determination with which those nail-pierced hands hold on to you. If it were possible for you and me to lose our salvation, we undoubtedly would have done so by now. But the gospel gives us a better word and a certain hope. The gospel is good news because Jesus definitely, certainly and eternally saves.

He is both the founder of our faith and the perfecter of our faith (Hebrews 12:2).

He is the Shepherd who comes after wandering sheep.

He is the Saviour who does not fail in his saving.

He is really, really good at what he does.

PRAY

Lord Jesus, I am so thankful that the gospel is true, that you are God, and that nothing can remove you from your throne or me from your love. I confess that you are not only the Saviour but that you are my Saviour. I am following you. I belong to you. And I believe that you will get me home. Amen.

*"The children of God are safe, again, not only because of the life they receive, but because of **the inner dangers which are averted**. Take the next sentence—'And they shall never perish'. They have a tendency to spiritual sickness, but their Shepherd will doctor them so that they shall never perish. They are sheep and have a tendency to wander, but their Shepherd shall keep them so that they shall never perish. Time tries them and they grow old, and the novelty of religion wears off, but they shall never perish ... The rule has absolutely no exception. The whole*

of them shall be preserved. Let them live to be as old as Methuselah, they shall never perish, whatever temptation may assail them. They may be tried, and troubled, and broken down, so that they may be hardly able to live, but they shall never perish. 'Never' is a long day, but it is not longer than grace will last. Blessed be God, this grand promise stands fast— 'They shall never perish'."

Charles Spurgeon, "The Security of Believers—or Sheep Who Shall Never Perish", Sermon #2120

CHAPTER 19

"I am the resurrection and the life"

READ JOHN 11:21-27

Jesus loved this family, and the apostle John explicitly tells us that (John 11:5). So when Jesus receives word that Lazarus is gravely ill, naturally we would expect to see him set off immediately to heal him. Yet this time, Jesus does the exact opposite, intentionally delaying his departure for another two days. By the time Jesus arrives at Bethany, Lazarus has already been dead for four days and is buried in a tomb (v 17).

We can palpably feel the sadness in Martha's voice upon his arrival. "Lord, if you had been here..." (v 21). Put yourself in her shoes for a moment. How long must every hour of those days have felt when Jesus did not turn up? The anxiety, as she laid her head on her pillow each evening, listening to Lazarus' condition deteriorate. The sorrow, as she buried her brother. The disappointment, as she went to bed that night—and on three further nights—knowing that Lazarus was dead and there was still no Jesus.

Maybe you've felt the same way with God's timing. Maybe you've come to God in similar frustration wondering, "Where were you? Why did you delay? Why weren't you there? Why did you let that happen?" Look at how Jesus responds to Martha. He doesn't rebuke her or chastise her. In fact, we later learn that he wept with her (v 35). God is not against humans experiencing the full range of their humanity through their emotions. In fact, judging by the kinds of prayers and songs throughout the book of Psalms, he welcomes it.

When Jesus tells Martha that her brother will indeed rise again, Martha mistakes it for him speaking eschatologically. That is, she thinks that he is speaking about the final resurrection on the day of judgment. And it is here that Jesus drops another of his "I am" statements, which reveal his identity. And I'd be lying if I didn't confess that this one is my personal favourite.

> *"I am the resurrection and the life. Whoever believes in me, though he die, yet shall he live, and everyone who lives and believes in me shall never die." (John 11:25-26)*

Jesus does not say that he merely *can* resurrect people and *can* give them life; resurrection and life is something that he *is*. For every other person in the history of the world, life is something that they *have* because it has been given to them. For Jesus, life is what he *is*. Jesus is saying to Martha that the last-day resurrection is not only a future event. It is someone here and now.

And Jesus asked her, "Do you believe this?" (v 26).

Martha's view of Jesus had been high. But it was not yet high enough. She saw him as a death-preventer, but not yet as the Death-Conqueror. But now, face to face with Life himself, she goes all in. "Yes, Lord; I believe that you are the Christ, the Son of God, who is coming into the world" (v 27). And as the story unfolds, the one who *is* life makes good on his promise, calling the four-day-dead Lazarus out of the tomb and back to life!

And within a matter of weeks from this extraordinary event, Jesus would face his own death. The one who is life would be crucified and buried in a tomb. Consider that for a moment: *Life himself would die.* And the disciples would all wonder, *Where are you, God? Why did you let that happen?* And like Jesus with Lazarus, God seemed to give no answer. But on the third day, at the appointed time, Jesus showed up and rose up with resurrection power! In that glorious moment, Jesus fulfilled his promises, validated his identity, reversed the curse of sin, and announced death's funeral.

And that's why Christians live differently in this world: they know that death does not get the final word. Not for Lazarus. Not for Jesus. And not for anyone who confesses with Martha, "Yes, Lord; I believe that you are the Christ". If Jesus, in whom you trust, is resurrection life, then that's *your* future. For the Christian, no longer is death a terrorist. It is now little more than a butler: opening the door for us into newness of life that will never erode. Whatever your present circumstances look like, his words speak to you today:

> *"I am the resurrection and the life. Whoever believes in me, though he die, yet shall he live, and everyone who lives and believes in me shall never die. Do you believe this?"*

PRAY

Lord Jesus, I long for the day when there are no more tears, no more sickness, no more sin, no more goodbyes and no more death. But I trust your timing. Give me the grace to wait well, to pray deeply, and to rejoice in the new life you've given me. I believe that you are the resurrection and the life. All my hope is in you. Amen.

> *"Remember how He said, 'I am the resurrection and the life'? Do not say, 'I believe in Christ and desire life'. You*

have it. Christ and life are not two things. He says, 'I am the resurrection and the life'. If you have Jesus Christ, you have the resurrection. Oh, that you might now realise what power lies in Him who is the resurrection and the life! All the power there is in Christ is there for His people. 'It pleased the Father that in Him should all fullness dwell,' and 'of His fullness have all we received'. Christ has a life in Himself, and He makes that life flow into every part of His mystical body according to His own word, 'Because I live, you shall live also'. Triumph, therefore, that you possess, as a believer this day, that same life which is inherent in the person of your glorious covenant Head."

Charles Spurgeon, "The Power of His Resurrection", Sermon #2080

CHAPTER 20

"Now is my soul troubled ... Father, glorify your name"

READ JOHN 12:23-28

*L*azarus had been raised from the dead, those who had witnessed the miracle had spread the word, and Jesus had been welcomed into Jerusalem with palm leaves and shouts of "Hosanna! Blessed is he who comes in the name of the Lord, even the King of Israel!" (John 12:12-18). Jesus' popularity had never been greater.

And yet Jesus was troubled.

What was it that troubled him? His hour had finally come (v 23). He had first spoken of this holy *hour* to his mother at a wedding in Cana (John 2:4), and he mentioned it repeatedly throughout his public ministry. It was the very reason he had come into the world: to be the once-and-for-all sacrifice for sin (Hebrews 9:11-12). Yet knowing why he had come did not lessen the magnitude of what he would have to endure. And he is honest about it.

"Now is my soul troubled..." (John 12:27)

Consider that for a moment. The one who is light and life, the one who created and upholds the universe, the one who powerfully commands the obedience of storms and demons alike with no more than his word... is troubled. His language is almost identical to that in David's prayer in Psalm 6:3: "My soul also is greatly troubled," which the CSB renders as, "My whole being is shaken with terror". Jesus is confessing that he is afraid.

Here we see the humanity of Jesus and a preview of the agonising prayer that would cause him to sweat blood in the Garden of Gethsemane a few days later. As the shadow of the cross loomed larger, there was an intensification of both holy anguish and singleness of purpose in Jesus' mind. He knew the Lamb of God had to suffer and die, but that is not what troubled him. It was more than mere physical agony, great as that would be, that troubled him. What filled his heart with dread was the "hour" in which he would become the bearer of sin and, therefore, separated from the Father.

For us to belong, Jesus had to be abandoned.

For us to be forgiven, Jesus had to be forsaken.

For us to be made whole, Jesus had to become the curse (Galatians 3:13).

Jesus was born to die, so that all who believe may be born again and never die. Consider what he says to his followers:

> *"Truly, truly, I say to you, unless a grain of wheat falls into the earth and dies, it reminds alone; but if it dies, it bears much fruit." (John 12:24)*

A seed has to die before it can produce a harvest of fruit, and so it was with Jesus. This is God's way: life comes *through* dying. There can be no resurrection without first a crucifixion, no glory without first suffering, no promised land without first a wilderness, no crown without first a cross. And as it was for Jesus, so it is for us:

> *"Whoever loves his life loses it, and whoever hates his life in*

*this world will keep it for eternal life. If anyone serves me,
he must follow me; and where I am, there will my servant
be also." (v 25-26)*

In other words, the only thing in all the world more costly
than following Jesus is… not. Hold on to your life and
you'll choke that life away. Release your life into the hands
of Jesus, by dying to your need to call the shots, and you'll
find more than everything you were ever looking for. It is
counterintuitive, but God has ordained freedom to come
through surrender and life to come through dying. And Jesus
wants to make sure that his disciples understand that he is
calling them to die to themselves and follow in his footsteps.

When someone asked George Müller, one of the most
fruitful and inspiring Christians of the 19th century, "What
has been the secret of your life?" Müller replied, "There was
a day when I died … died to George Müller, his opinions,
preferences, tastes, and will; died to the world, its approval
or censure; died to the approval or blame even of brethren or
friends."[14]

Facing the greatest trial any human would ever endure, how
does Jesus answer the anguish within his soul? He dies before
he dies. He reminds himself that it was for this hour that he
had come into the world. Then he prays, "Father, glorify your
name" (v 28). Jesus empties his very real anxieties into the
hands of the Father's very real sovereignty. This battle would
be repeated days later in Gethsemane with an even greater
turmoil within. And yet again, he would conclude, "Not my
will, but yours, be done" (Luke 22:42).

That's where Jesus wants us to go as well. To be honest with
God about what worries us and then to bring it to him in
prayer. To follow Jesus with confidence into the Father's bank

---

14 R. Kent Hughes, *John: That You May Believe* (Crossway Books, 1999),
p 301.

of infinite grace and cash in your every anxiety for prayerful rest. To say, "Though this troubles me, though my heart is unsettled, Father, I trust you. Be glorified in my life."

REFLECT

Think about what weighs you down with anxiety right now. Where do you need to follow Jesus' example of speaking honestly to God about your troubles? Take a moment and tell him how you feel. Name those troubles to him now, "casting all your anxieties on him, because he cares for you" (1 Peter 5:7), and then ask that he would glorify his name in every one of them.

"A child may have lost its way, and it may be sobbing its heart out in its distress, but the moment it sees its father, it is lost no longer, it has found its way, and is at rest. Though there may be no difference in your position, nor change in your circumstances, yet if you catch a sight of your heavenly Father, it is enough. You are a lost child no more. When you can pray, 'Father, glorify your name,' then there is no more question about, 'What shall I say?' You have said the right thing and there let it end ... If you can pray in that fashion, your confidence will come back to you; if you have been greatly distracted, calm peace will visit you again, for now you will say, 'I will bear the Lord's will, and will be content therewith. I cannot quarrel with my Master's dealings any more, for I have asked Him to glorify His name, and as I know that He is doing it, I cannot murmur. How can I struggle against that which is really glorifying my Father?' Your heart will cease to question and to quake, and nestle down beneath the eternal wings, in deep and happy peace."

Charles Spurgeon, "A Golden Prayer", Sermon #1391

CHAPTER 21

"If I do not wash you..."

READ JOHN 13:1-9

*I*f you knew you only had one night left on earth, and you're anything like me, it's probably fair to say that "foot washing" wouldn't make the bucket list of how you wanted to use those precious final hours. But on the eve of his crucifixion—the greatest act of sacrificial love the world would ever see—Jesus visibly demonstrates to his disciples what he had earlier taught them:

> *"Whoever would be great among you must be your servant, and whoever would be first among you must be slave of all. For even the Son of Man came not to be served but to serve, and to give his life as a ransom for many."*
>
> *(Mark 10:43-45)*

Humility is the way of the kingdom of Jesus. The greatness that Christians are to aspire to is the greatness of servanthood that Jesus himself embraced. The surprising glory that marked his first night in this world—as he entered humanity via the humility of a dirty manger—would be the same type of glory that would mark his final night, as he washed the dirty feet of eleven disciples and one traitor. It is the glory of stooping.

And by the same time the following evening, Jesus would have stooped even lower in sacrificial love. By the same time the next day, his body—whipped and broken and pierced and bloody—would have been carried lifeless down from the cross and laid in a rich man's tomb. This is what John meant when he said, "Having loved his own who were in the world, he loved them to the end" (John 13:1).

But that's tomorrow. Tonight, he still has much he wants to teach them. In fact, the next five chapters of John's Gospel (13 – 17) are exclusively dedicated to the instruction and prayers of Jesus for his followers. Yet before the Passover meal begins, Jesus rises from the table, strips down to his underwear and ties a towel around his waist. He *literally* takes the form of a servant. And he makes his way around the room with a basin of water, washing the feet of these men—feet caked with dust and dirt and everything else that a sandal-wearing people in an agrarian culture would have picked up after a day of travelling on foot. The way John tells the story seems to imply that each of these men are stunned into silence.

Everyone, except Peter (no surprise there!). Peter recoils and cries, "Lord, do you wash my feet? … You shall never wash my feet!" (13:6, 8, emphasis added). His shock at the thought of the Messiah performing such a humiliating act of service for him personally is a commendable theological instinct. *That's not the way this is meant to work Jesus! Humanity serves God, not the other way around. What kind of Messiah—what kind of King—does servant-work? This doesn't make any sense!* Peter was right to think this was all backward and undeserved. But that's what grace is.

Jesus looks at Peter and says, "If I do not wash you, you have no share with me" (v 8). You see, Jesus was giving more than just an example of servanthood that he called his followers to walk in. He was foreshadowing the spiritual cleansing that was about to come through the shedding of his blood, prophesied in Isaiah 1:18: "Though your sins are like scarlet, they shall be as white as snow". If Jesus had said, "Unless you prove yourself worthy, unless you show yourself to be a morally impressive person—unless you *clean up your act*—you have no share with me," then Christianity would not be good news at all. But Jesus says, in effect, "*I* must wash *you*." How humbling. The only thing we contribute to our salvation is the outstretched dirty feet.

Where do we find the power to live lives marked by the greatness of servanthood? Only by looking again and again and again to what we ourselves have received from Jesus. Your ability to extend grace to and serve others around you is directly proportional to your awareness of how greatly Jesus has shown grace to you and served you—and how he continues to do so.

If *Jesus* washed the feet of his disciples, then none of his disciples are above serving others. And if Jesus washed the feet of his own *betrayer*, then there is no one you know in this world who is beneath being served. So let's embrace the glory of stooping, pressing onward to the day when we hear those precious words from our Saviour, "Well done, good and faithful servant" (Matthew 25:21).

REFLECT
Think about the people you are planning to see over the next few days. How might those interactions with your family, friends, and co-workers look if you were to approach them with the foot-washing example of Jesus seared into your heart?

"The Lord Jesus loves His people so, that every day He is washing their feet. Their poorest action He accepts. Their

deepest sorrow He feels. Their smallest wish He hears, and their greatest sin He forgives. He is still their servant as well as their friend. Still He takes the basin. Still He wears the towel ... Remember that Christ's way of rising is to go down. He descended, that He might ascend. And so must we. Let us count that evermore it is our highest honour and our greatest glory to lay aside all honour and all glory and to win honour and glory out of shame and humiliation for Christ Jesus' sake."

Charles Spurgeon, "Jesus Washing His Disciples' Feet", Sermon #612

CHAPTER 22

"By this all will know you are my disciples"

READ JOHN 13:12-15, 34-35

*A*fter washing the feet of his friends, Jesus expanded on what this attitude was to look like among the disciples once he had left them. What they saw him do for them, they were to imitate and do for one another. "For I have given you an example, that you also should do just as I have done to you" (John 13:15). I can't help but wonder if this living parable was one of the primary images imprinted on the disciples' memories—an image that energised their ministry for the rest of their lives. After all, each of them would spend the rest of their years serving God's people and sacrificially taking the gospel across the known world. I wonder how many times when they were weary of doing good, or felt entitlement creeping into their hearts, or were just not in the mood, that the Spirit brought this scene to the forefront of their minds, along with their Saviour's words: "Do just as I have done to you".

Then Jesus adds: *"A new commandment I give to you"* (v 34).

Clearly this is not a suggestion or an option or an interesting spiritual insight or an elite-level discipleship pathway for the super-committed. This command is the life-reorienting description, directly from the King, of what his kingdom will look like.

In the same way that the earth orbits the sun, his followers were to bend the entirety of their lives around what he was about to say. This really matters to Jesus. To him, anything less than this does not qualify as authentic Christianity.

"Just as I have loved you, you also are to love one another."
(v 34)

At first glance, this doesn't really seem all that "new". Hadn't Jesus already taught that the second-greatest command after loving God was to "love your neighbour as yourself" (Luke 10:27)? Yes—but what makes the command in John 13 *new* is that Jesus is raising the bar. Previously Jesus had said that we are to love others—even our enemies (Matthew 5:44)—as much as we love ourselves. But here he is calling Christians to love *one another* as much as *he loves them*, which is a far greater love. On the cross, Jesus loved us *more* than he loved himself, and he proved it by laying down his life for us. He is saying, in effect, *The way in which you have been loved by me, and the intensity with which you have been loved by me, is how you are to treat one another.*

Then in the next breath, he shows why this matters.

"By this all people will know that you are my disciples, if you have love for one another." (John 13:35)

This is incredible. The way in which we make the gospel credible to unbelievers around us is not primarily through the depth of our love for Jesus but through our love for one another. When we love God first and most (again, see Luke 10:27), that is not surprising to the world. Unbelievers expect believers to be devoted to their God. What surprises the world is when Christians love one another with the same earnest constancy that Christ loved them. That's unexpected. This kind of love, displayed in our life together, becomes a living apologetic. So much so that Francis Schaeffer points out:

> *"If an individual Christian does not show love toward other*
> *true Christians, the world has a right to judge that he [or*
> *she] is not a Christian. Here Jesus is stating something*
> *else which is much more cutting, much more profound:*
> *We cannot expect the world to believe that the Father sent*
> *the Son, that Jesus' claims are true, and that Christianity*
> *is true, unless the world sees some reality of the oneness of*
> *true Christians."* [15]

In other words, the world will know that our good news is true news by the beauty of our love for one other. Relational beauty in your church is the *sina qua non*—the indispensable ingredient—of authentic Christianity. That means that every time you gather with other Christians for Sunday worship, or in smaller groups throughout the week, your presence and intentionality and words and actions are indispensably vital to the credibility of your church, because the best argument for the gospel is not a concept but a community. Not passionate eloquence but ordinary people who, in the midst of a divided world, love well. What else would we want to be known for? In light of what matters so much to Jesus, let's not hold back from each other. Consider how you might love your own church particularly, and the wider Christian body generally, with Christ-like intensity over the coming months.

> *"Just as I have loved you, you also are to love one another.*
> *By this all people will know that you are my disciples, if*
> *you have love for one another."*

---

15 Francis Schaeffer, *The Mark of the Christian* (InterVarsity Press, 1970), p 15.

PRAY

Lord Jesus, as I think about how unsparingly you have loved me, I want to love my brothers and sisters in the same way. I want to love more earnestly. Show me where I can do that. Deepen the affections of those in our church for one another and make us a credible witness to your saving love to those around us. Amen.

"It is a very blessed thing when we are able to love one another, because the grace that is in any one of us sees the grace that is in another, and discerns in that other, not the flesh and blood of the Saviour, but such a resemblance to Christ that it must love that other one for His sake. As it is true that, if we are of the world, the world will love its own, so is it true that if we are of the Spirit, the Spirit will love His own. The whole redeemed family of Christ is firmly bound together. Born of God ourselves, we keep looking out to see others who have been 'born again, not of corruptible seed, but of incorruptible'. And when we do see them, we cannot help loving them. There is a bond of union between us at once ... It will be one of the clearest evidences to your own heart that you are really a disciple of Jesus when you realise that, for Christ's sake, you love the whole redeemed family of God. By this test shall all men know that you are His disciples and you shall begin by knowing it yourself."

Charles Spurgeon, "Christ's New Commandment", Sermon #2936

CHAPTER 23

"I go to prepare a place for you"

READ JOHN 14:1-3

*A*t a glance, Jesus seems to be saying that he is going away and intends to spend his time in heaven preparing wonderful accommodations for his people. It's as if Jesus, the one-time earthly carpenter, is promising to pick up his divine hammer and renovate the heavenly Airbnb for his followers before they arrive there. But that is not quite what is going on here.

Only hours away from betrayal and death, Jesus, in his final discourse with his disciples, wants to fill their hearts with courage through his promises. Moments earlier he had said to them, "Little children, yet a little while I am with you. You will seek me, and just as I said to the Jews, so now I also say to you, 'Where I am going you cannot come'" (John 13:33). What does he mean by this? Where is Jesus going to go, that his people cannot go as well? He cannot mean death, since every believer will still die. And in this verse he cannot be referring to heaven, since every believer will indeed eventually be with him there.

Where Jesus was going, where no one else can go—and no one ever again need go—was to the cross. It is by his death that Jesus prepares a place for us in his Father's house (14:2).

Only Jesus was able to go to the cross as the sacrificial Lamb, "who takes away the sin of the world" (John 1:29). Only Jesus loved us so much that he took our place as "the atoning sacrifice for our sins" (1 John 4:10, CSB). Only Jesus was able willingly to enter underneath the righteous judgment of God and come out the other side vindicated and unscathed, beaming with resurrection glory.

So this can't be a passage about what Jesus intended to do for us *after* he got to heaven. He was talking about what he intended to do *in order to* get us to heaven.

And here, we see again the lengths that Jesus will go to not only save his people but to give them assurance that he really has done it all.

Maybe you still have questions that linger...

Do you feel morally under-qualified for entry into the Father's presence? You are. But Jesus is not looking at your résumé; he wants you to trust in his. *"Let not your heart be troubled. Believe in ... me"* (John 14:1).

Do you ever wonder if your name might not have made the divine list? If there is no room for you in the Father's house? Jesus wants you to know there is room for you. In fact, the breadth of God's saving love is wider than you think (Ephesians 3:18-19), and the Father's house has *many* rooms (John 14:2). The one word "many" is there to "deepen our confidence in the triumphs of Christ's Cross".[16] Jesus will not fail at a single point in his work as the Saviour.

Does a haunting doubt sometimes creep into the corners of your heart: you think that because of your present sin, Jesus is perhaps going to change his mind about you? Does the presence of a personal wilderness season seem to you evidence that God has abandoned you? Bury the thought for

---

16 Alexander Maclaren, *Expositions of Holy Scripture: St John Chapters I-XIV* (Eerdmans, 1938), p 268.

ever! There is a greater chance of you extinguishing the light of the sun with a water pistol than there is of Jesus failing to complete the work he began in you (Philippians 1:6).

So when Jesus says, "If I go and prepare a place for you, I will come again and will take you to myself" (John 14:3), he is saying, *If I am willing to go to the cross for you, if I am willing to bear the punishment of your sins for you, if I am willing to go to such lengths to prepare a room for you in my Father's house, I most certainly will not abandon you along the way!*

The reason your heart need not be troubled is because Jesus faced your greatest trouble. He has reserved a place in the Father's house for you and for all who believe in him, with the most precious currency in all the universe: *his own blood.* And if your greatest trouble is already in your rear-vision mirror, then you need never wonder if he will overlook you in any of your lesser troubles that lie along the narrow path to glory. So press on with the confidence that not only has Jesus prepared a place for you; he is this very moment at work in you through every trial and trouble, preparing you for that place.

PRAY

Jesus, there is nothing I more need to know right now than the certainty of your love for me. Thank you for preparing a place for me in the Father's house. Help me to see today what you have secured for me eternally.

"*The place is prepared; are you prepared for it? Do you believe on the Lord Jesus Christ? If so, your preparation has begun. Do you love the Lord and love His people? If so, your preparation is going on. Do you hate sin and do you pant after holiness? If so, your preparation is progressing.*

*Are you nothing at all and is Jesus Christ your All-in-all?
Then you are almost ready, and may the Lord keep you in
that condition, and before long, swing up the gates of pearl
and let you into the prepared place. May the Lord bring us
all safely there, for Jesus' sake! Amen."*

Charles Spurgeon, "A Prepared Place for a Prepared People",
Sermon #2751

CHAPTER 24

"You still do not know me?"

READ JOHN 14:6-9

*I*n this passage we are often (and rightly) drawn to Jesus' statement of exclusivity in John 14:6. He is not *a* way among many but *the* way. He is not *a* truth but the embodiment of *the* truth. There is only one way to the Father, and that is through Jesus alone.

But can I draw your eyes to the question in verse 9? In curious exasperation, Philip responds to Jesus' claim with the request, "Lord, show us the Father, and [that will be] enough for us" (v 8). In other words, Philip wants it to be irrefutably clear: *We've seen your miracles and heard your words and believe that you're the promised Messiah. But can you convince us one more time?* He's asking Jesus to settle the matter once and for all.

And Jesus looks at him and responds with a gentle yet chiding question. I can imagine him shaking his head, smiling but with a hint of sadness embedded into the smile. The kind that creeps into the corners of the eyes. Like the face of a patient friend who keeps showing up for you after you made a mess of things again. Like that of a parent whose stressed-out teenager just shouted, "You don't know what I'm going through!" because they have a big assignment due the next day. Like that of the Saviour who knows that tomorrow he will do the blood-spilling work of his saving.

> *"Have I been with you so long, and you still do not know me, Philip?" (v 9)*

You see, this is why Jesus came: so that we may know him. Do you know him?

An exercise I'll often do when reading Scripture is to emphasise a different word in the phrase or sentence I'm mulling over. It's like turning around a beautiful gem and watching it catch the light from various angles. Why don't you take a few moments and slowly turn those four words over in your mind?

> Do you know *Jesus?*
> Do you *know* Jesus?
> Do *you* know Jesus?

To not know him, or to pretend to know him, is the greatest of dangers. At the end of his famous Sermon on the Mount in Matthew 7:21-23, Jesus warns that there will be "many" who claim to have prophesied in his name, cast out demons in his name, and done many great works in his name. And on the final day, Jesus will say to them, "I never knew you; depart from me, you workers of lawlessness" (v 23). Not that he had known them once upon a time and then something came along and severed their relationship. Jesus says of these people that he *never* knew them, and therefore they never truly knew him. You see, it is possible to know a lot about Jesus and not know Jesus. It is possible to do a lot for Jesus and not know Jesus.

Yet to truly know him is the greatest of all joys and most precious of all treasures. It is why God said through the prophet Jeremiah, "Let not the wise man boast in his wisdom, let not the mighty man boast in his might, let not the rich man boast in his riches, but let him who boasts boast in this, that he understands and knows me" (Jeremiah 9:23-24). Is there anything greater? When all is said and done, only one thing matters.

Do you know him?

Here's one way we can be sure that we *do* know Jesus: we long to know him *more*. Our hearts say with the apostle Paul—who, after enjoying, worshipping and faithfully serving Jesus for around three decades, near the end of his life declared this—"My goal is to know him and the power of his resurrection and the fellowship of his sufferings" (Philippians 3:10, CSB). For to know him and be known by him is the ultimate relational reality, which we will spend all of eternity marvelling over and delighting in. And it is a gift not only for your future but for this very moment—right now, right where you are.

PRAY

Jesus, open the eyes of my heart to what I most need today. And that need is to know a little more of you. Actually, a lot more of you. Beholding you and enjoying you is what I most long for. To walk increasingly closer to you is the great, all-satisfying goal of my life. Amen.

"Full many a time I have heard the Master's voice in
the inner chambers of my heart, expostulating with me
thus—'Have I been so long time with thee, and hast thou
not known Me?' And then I have said, 'Alas! Lord, I have
not known Thee as I should, and I feel that I cannot
know Thee as I would.' Come, beloved, let us talk it over

together. Sometimes, in deep quietude of spirit, our heart has been giving itself to devotion; it may have been a time of suffering. The world was all shut out, and sweetly did our soul begin to perceive the love and the loveliness of Christ, till the vision of the Saviour grew clearer and brighter, and more brilliant still ... May you go on further and further learning of Christ, making discoveries of His glory till you shall be with Him where he is, to behold that glory, and to be participators in it. God bless you at this feast of His love. May He be present with us to make glad our hearts! Amen."

Charles Spurgeon, "Chiding and Cheering", Sermon #3430

CHAPTER 25

"The ruler of this world has no claim on me"

READ JOHN 14:27-31

*I*f you are weary and need hope or if you are overwhelmed and need courage, John 14 is the right chapter to turn to. Jesus repeatedly meets the anxious uncertainty and fear of the future that had crept into the hearts of his disciples with assurance after assurance that he is not abandoning them. That they can bank on his promises. That everything is unfolding just as the Father purposed it.

> *"Let not your hearts be troubled." (v 27)*
> *"I will come to you." (v 28)*
> *"I have told you before it takes place, so that when it does … you may believe." (v 29)*

Over and over, Jesus brings their worries into the light of his divine identity and definite plan: a plan that no human, government, force or devil can thwart. And it is to this last potential enemy—"the ruler of this world" (v 30)—that Jesus turns their attention and gives them a reason to trust him.

> *"The ruler of this world is coming. He has no claim on me."*

Think about that for a moment. Like a volcano on the brink of exploding, the pent-up rage of Satan, which has been boiling across the centuries, is about to be unleashed upon Jesus. The full force of hell has been aimed at him. The ruler of this world has squared his feet and is about to throw his hardest punch. For tonight is the night when the first prophecy will become present reality, as the ancient serpent is permitted to strike and bruise the promised one's heel (Genesis 3:15).

And here's what Jesus wants his disciples to know: Satan will lose. *He has no claim on me.*

The phrase Jesus uses here is one frequently found within a legal setting: if an accuser had failed to present credible evidence of a crime, the defendant could say, "He's got nothing on me!" Yet Jesus' claim is even greater: Satan has no claim *on* him because there is no sin *in* him.

Who but Jesus could something like that be said of?

Point to any other person in the history of the world and Satan would have a field day with the evidence he could present. Line up Adam and Eve, Abraham and Sarah, Moses, John Calvin, Mother Teresa, Billy Graham, you, me and all the rest in the courtroom of God's justice, and not one of us will be walking out of there with a "not-guilty" verdict once the accuser has finished with us.

But Jesus says, *"He has no claim on me".*

For while even the best of us are yet stained with sin, Jesus alone is the sacrificial "lamb without blemish or spot" (1 Peter 1:19). And he has cleared our debt with the only currency of any value in the courtroom of God: the testimony of his own precious blood.

And here's where this good news gets just downright astonishing. If you are in Christ Jesus, united to him not by your moral record but by faith in his, then the ruler of this world has no claim on you either. You need not fear the bite of the serpent who struck Christ's heel, for his fangs were shattered in the process. You need not lose sleep over the accusations shot at you by the ruler of this world, even though every one of them be true!

For, as the apostle Paul declares in Colossians 2:13-14, God has forgiven you of every one of them, "by cancelling the record of debt that stood against [you] with its legal demands. This he set aside, nailing it to the cross." And when he did, he disarmed the devil of all his accusing power, publicly shaming him through the triumph of Jesus over him (v 15). And now, every Christian can appropriate their Saviour's own words with confidence and declare of their accuser, "*He has no claim on me*".

PRAY

Jesus, you are a perfect Saviour, and your righteousness is a perfect righteousness. I remember today that my trust is not in my record but in yours, and my hope is not in my obedience but in yours. Satan has no claim on me. Not now, not ever. Because my life is hidden in yours. And my future is sure.

"And now, what says this to us? Simply this. If Christ on the cross has spoiled Satan, let us not be afraid to encounter this great enemy of our souls. My brethren, in all things we must be made like unto Christ. We must bear our cross, and on that cross we must fight as He did with sin, and death, and hell. Let us not fear. The result of the battle is certain, for as the Lord our Saviour has overcome once even so shall we most surely conquer in Him. Be you none of you afraid with sudden fear when the evil one comes upon you. If he accuse you, reply to him in these words—'Who shall lay anything to the charge of God's elect?' ... If death should threaten you, shout in his very face—'O Grave!

Where is thy sting? O death! Where is thy victory?' Hold up the cross before you. Let that be your shield and buckler, and rest assured that as your Master not only routed the foe but afterwards took the spoil, it shall be even so with you."

Charles Spurgeon, "Christ Triumphant", Sermon #273

CHAPTER 26

"Abide in me"

READ JOHN 15:4-5

Where is home for you?
What comes into your mind when you dwell on that word for a few moments?

Home.

In its most basic sense, home is simply where one lives. But more than that, a healthy home is a place of refuge from the chaos around us. It is a place of belonging where we can enter and exhale. Home greets us at the end of a workday like a Labrador that is ever consistent in its readiness to welcome us in and delight in our presence.

While many of us may have experienced the uncertainty that comes from growing up in a broken family or navigating a nomadic childhood, in which we constantly moved about (seven schools in twelve years for me personally), there is still a longing deep in all of us that the word "home" awakens in our hearts. *Home* whispers to us the possibility of permanence.

That's what Jesus means when he says, "Abide in me" (John 15:4). To abide means to stay. To put down roots. To make your home there. Branches don't bear fruit if they're not abiding in the vine. And the same is true for Christians. In fact, Jesus could not be clearer: "I am the vine; you are the branches ... apart from me you can do nothing" (v 5). Notice how all-important our union with Christ is. Apart from Jesus, we are not *less* fruitful; we are *not* fruitful. In other words, Jesus doesn't want your strength. He wants you to stay close to him so that he can give you his.

And this means that real Christianity is not a self-improvement project of constant striving, nor is it a *laissez-faire* attitude of passive waiting. Real Christianity is nothing less than a supernatural union, whereby we make our home in Christ ("abide in me") because Christ has made his home in us ("and I in you"). And fruit is what results.

Such a staggering reality completely changes how you live today as far as your discipleship to Jesus is concerned. Your immediate goal today, then, is not to try and be *like* Jesus. That's the outcome—the inevitable by-product if you like. Your immediate goal today is to be *with* Jesus.

To walk with him.

To make your home in him.

To live your life in conscious proximity to him.

"Abide in me."

And as you do that, Jesus promises that your life *will* bear "much fruit" (v 5). The process of becoming like Jesus is a daily, Spirit-empowered reorienting of our eyes back to him. How could it be otherwise? As Paul writes in 2 Corinthians 3:18, "And we all, with unveiled face, beholding the glory of the Lord, are being transformed into the same image from one degree of glory to another. For this comes from the Lord who is the Spirit." When "Christ-with-ness" is our daily goal, Christ-likeness will be the outcome.

If Jesus is our true home, in whom we have refuge and permanence and delight and love and life, then the primary question facing you today is one of location: *Where will you live?* Like a restless 15-year-old, wanting to flex our independence and demonstrate our self-sufficiency, we too have a tendency to forget how good our home really is. But you don't have to go searching for love or life or anything else anymore. They're already yours in Christ.

As the author G.K. Chesterton put it, "There are two ways of getting home; and one of them is to stay there. The other is to walk round the whole world till we come back to the same place."[17]

So where will you live today?

Jesus says, *"Abide in me."*

PRAY

Thank you, Jesus, that you are the true vine and you have grafted my life into yours. Help me not to look elsewhere for what I already have in you. You are my home. Where you are is where I want to be. Today I ask that you fill me with your fullness and let your life flow through me. Amen.

> *"Though without Him you can do nothing, yet with Him all things are possible! Omnipotence is in that man who has Christ in him! Weakness, itself, you may be, but you shall learn to glory in that weakness because the power of Christ rests upon you if your union and communion with Christ are continually kept up! Oh for a grand confidence in Christ! ... Oh for the splendour of the faith which measures itself by the Christ in whom it trusts! May God bring us there! Then shall we bring forth much fruit to the glory of His name."*

Charles Spurgeon, "Without Christ—Nothing", Sermon #1625

---

17 G.K. Chesterton, *The Everlasting Man* (Hodder & Stoughton, 1927), p 9.

CHAPTER 27

"I have called you friends"

READ JOHN 15:12-15

*A*mong the circle of wonderfully different and precious people whom I get to call my friends, none have taught me more *about* friendship than Alex. Fiercely loyal and joyful, he holds a doctorate and a boatload of childlike wonder—along with a healthy dash of craziness. He is deeply committed to delighting in Jesus and each relationship that God has given him. Everyone needs a friend like Alex. Once when he got word that I was navigating an incredibly difficult and complicated leadership crisis, I got a voice message from him saying, "Hey. Are you in trouble? I will get on the next airplane and be wherever I need to be. Whatever you need. All that's mine is yours, I've got your back no matter what. I love you, Adam."

That's a true friend. Not many people will drop everything and fly across the world for you. Fewer still will lay down their life for you. Yet according to Jesus, this is what true love and real friendship look like: "Greater love has no one than this, that someone lay down his life for his friends" (John 15:13). And that's precisely the category Jesus puts us in. On the night before his crucifixion, Jesus looks around the room into eleven pairs of eyes and says:

"You are my friends…" (John 15:14)

Is there any greater privilege in the world than to have Jesus—the Word-become-flesh, the Creator and Sustainer of all, the King over every other king and Lord above every other Lord—look at you and say, *"You are my friend"*? Those words are the knockout blow to both self-promotion and self-loathing because in the friendship of Jesus, our deepest needs—of being fully known and yet fully loved—are fully satisfied.

In fact, it's a statement so glorious and captivating that Jesus could ask anything of us, and our hearts would leap at the opportunity to reciprocate such love, right? Well, that's exactly what he does do.

"You are my friends if you do what I command you." (v 14)

Jesus is not suggesting that obedience is what earns his friendship but that obedience is what evidences his friendship. His heart, which delights in the Father's will, has become our heart. It's not that he stops being our Lord and King. Not at all. It's that he gives us both instruction *and* intimacy. A servant receives the first, but only a friend is invited into the second. Which is why he says, "I have called you friends, for all that I have heard from my Father I have made known to you" (v 15).

Yet there is something specific here that Jesus is commanding of his disciples. Something that above all else proves we have really received his grace and entered into friendship with him. He tells us explicitly in verse 12:

"This is my commandment, that you love one another as I have loved you."

Jesus is restating what he had said to the disciples earlier that night: the love that he has shown them, and will show them, through the laying down of his life for them is to be the love demonstrated among them. "A new commandment I give to you, that you love one another: just as I have loved you, you also are to love one another" (13:34). Because sacrificial love is the defining characteristic of true friendship, it is to be the unmistakable practice of all who claim to be friends of Jesus.

Tertullian, a leader within the early church, remarked that the Roman world looked at Christians and exclaimed, "See how these Christians love one another; they are even ready to die for one another!" The watching world's incredulity was not due to the intellectual prowess or miraculous feats or organisational impressiveness of the church but to what Jesus is talking about here in John 15: their love for one another. Imagine if your church became known as a community of people who loved like this. Who say to one another, like my friend Alex said to me, "Whatever you need. I've got your back. I love you." Who among your brothers and sisters in Christ might need you to be that kind of friend to them right now?

"Greater love has no one than this, that someone lay down his life for his friends." (v 13)

This is Christianity. It is how Jesus has loved you; he loves in a way that holds nothing back. And when we truly see how greatly we have been loved by him, our heart's desire is to go and do likewise.

PRAY

Jesus, as you have been to me, I want to be to others. To be called your friend is the greatest privilege of my life. Where I have been holding back in my love for others out of self-protection or self-centredness, forgive me and help me to love as you love. I want to be the friend to others that you are to me.

*"Beloved, I cannot tell you all that Christ has done for sinners, but this I know—if He meets with you tonight, and becomes your friend, He will stand by you to the last ... You shall be hard at work tomorrow, but as you wipe the sweat from your brow, He shall stand by you. You will, perhaps, be despised for His sake, but He will not forsake you; you will, perhaps, have days of sickness, but He will come and make your bed in your sickness for you. You will, perhaps, be poor, but your bread shall be given you, and your water shall be sure, for He will provide for you. You will vex Him much and grieve His Spirit. You will often doubt Him—you will go after other lovers; you will provoke Him to jealousy, but He will never cease to love you. You will, perhaps, grow cold to Him, and even forget His dear name for a time, but He will never forget you. You may, perhaps, dishonour His cross, and damage His fair fame among the sons of men, but He will never cease to love you. No, He will never love you less—He cannot love you more ... And when the splendours of the millennium shall come, you shall partake of them—when the end shall be, and the world shall be rolled up like a worn-out vesture, and these arching skies shall have passed away like a forgotten dream—when eternity, with its deep-sounding waves, shall break up on the rocks of time, and sweep them away forever—then, on that sea of glass mingled with fire you shall stand with Christ, **your friend still**, claiming you, notwithstanding all your misbehaviour in the world which has gone, and loving you now, loving you on as long as eternity shall last! Oh, what a friend is Christ to sinners!"*

Charles Spurgeon, "The Sinner's Friend", Sermon #556

CHAPTER 28

"I chose you"

READ JOHN 15:16-19

*E*veryone in the room with Jesus on his final night knew that they were ultimately there because of one deciding factor. It was not because they had taken the initiative with Jesus but because Jesus had taken the initiative with them.

> *"You did not choose me, but I chose you and appointed you." (John 15:16)*

What a humbling truth. Every one of us who has received God's grace knows that we have done absolutely nothing to deserve it. He did not choose us because of our merits but because of his mercy. Not because we are so lovely but because he is so loving. The impact of his words to Israel in Deuteronomy 7:7-8 are no less profound to every one of us in Christ today: "It was not because you were more in number than any other people that the Lord set his love on you and chose you, for you were the fewest of all peoples, but it is because the Lord loves you."

Yet, as the scholar Frederick Bruner points out—and as each of these disciples would soon find out—to be chosen by Jesus was not only a great privilege but "the beginning of a great persecution."[18]

---

18 Frederick Dale Bruner, *The Gospel of John: A Commentary* (Eerdmans, 2012), p 903.

"If you were of the world, the world would love you as its own; but because you are not of the world, but I chose you out of the world, therefore the world hates you."

(John 15:19)

In one sense, Jesus here is giving his followers an accurate expectation for their earthly experience of following him. And he doesn't mince words. The world will hate you. You see, to be at home with Jesus means being exiled by the world. And to be a friend of Jesus means being seen as an enemy by the world. This is why Peter—who himself was no stranger to suffering for Christ's sake—addresses his letter to the churches of his time with the opening words, "To those chosen, living as exiles" (1 Peter 1:1, CSB). "Chosen" reminds us of how undeservedly loved we are by Jesus. "Exiles" reminds us of how hated we will be because of that. In the Old Testament, God's people were sometimes exiled because of their disobedience to God. But in the New Testament, God's people will be exiled because of their obedience to God.

Has Jesus chosen you out of the world by pouring his love into your heart? Then just accept it already: you're not cool; you're a Christian. Why spend another second worrying about an acceptance from others that you can only have by rejecting Jesus? The only way the world will love you is if you belong to them. Yet the moment you quit trying to impress the unbelieving world is the precise moment you are free to start loving them and serving them as Jesus would have you do. So think about it: whose opinions are you enslaved to? To the degree we need the world's acceptance, we will be paralysed by a fear of the world's rejection. Yet to the degree we are convinced that we've been chosen, called and loved by Jesus, we will embrace the cost of following in his footsteps.

We Christians should be the last people to go looking for trouble. But neither should we be shocked when it turns up on our doorstep. Jesus said that it would. Francis George—a cardinal in the archdiocese of Chicago—captured the posture that we ought to adopt when it comes to our expectations of a hostile world. He once said:

> *"I [expect] to die in bed, my successor will die in prison and his successor will die a martyr in the public square ... His successor will pick up the shards of a ruined society and slowly help rebuild civilization, as the church has done so often in human history."*[19]

We've been chosen by grace. And we've been chosen to be agents of grace. Let's embrace both the privileges and the persecution, knowing in whose footsteps we are following. And when persecution comes—when the world hates you— you won't be "surprised at the fiery trial when it comes upon you to test you, as though something strange were happening to you" (1 Peter 4:12). Instead, you can live with the confidence that "after you have suffered a little while, the God of all grace, who has called you to his eternal glory in Christ, will himself restore, confirm, strengthen, and establish you" (5:10).

You belong to Jesus. You've been appointed by him for fruitfulness in him. He will surely be with you through whatever he calls you to endure for his sake.

PRAY

"Father, when life hurts the most, remind us in our heart of hearts that you are the 'God of all grace'—the one who has called us to 'eternal glory'—and that you will most definitely 'restore, confirm, strengthen, and establish' us. Make your word more real than our pain. Make your grace more substantive than our sufferings. Grant us, like Paul, the joyful assurance

---

19 Francis George, https://www.ncregister.com/blog/cardinal-george-the-myth-and-reality-of-ill-die-in-my-bed (accessed April 4, 2022).

that 'the glory that is to be revealed to us' (Romans 8:18) will make all the sufferings of our brief journey in this world seem like feathers compared to the weight of eternal goodness that will be lavished on us when Jesus returns. Hallelujah! Until that day, grant us grace to steward our pain as a gift, making us more compassionate and merciful to others. We pray in Jesus' faithful and beautiful name. Amen."[20]

*"Man chooses those who would be most helpful to him. God chooses those to whom He can be the most helpful. We select those who may give us the best return. God frequently selects those who most **need** His aid. … It is the very opposite way of choosing. We select those who are best because they are most deserving. God selects those who are worst because they are least deserving, so that His choice may be more clearly seen to be an act of grace and not of merit."*

Charles Spurgeon, "God's Strange Choice", Sermon #587

---

20 Scotty Smith, *Every Season Prayers: Gospel-Centered Prayers for the Whole of Life* (Baker Books, 2016), p 53.

CHAPTER 29

"It is to your advantage
that I go away"

READ JOHN 16:6-7

*B*e honest. Sometimes, like me, you read Jesus' words recorded for us in Scripture and think to yourself, "Really? Are you sure, Jesus?" Maybe you don't say it out loud, but the thought is there, right? Today's passage is one of those occasions when we encounter words that are hard to hear because, as it turns out, we are far more like the disciples than perhaps we'd like to admit.

Looking around the room at his heavy-hearted friends, who are processing all that he has told them so far—his final instructions, promises and warnings of future persecution—Jesus then says:

> "Nevertheless, I tell you the truth: it is to your advantage
> that I go away..." (John 16:7)

Put yourself in their sandals for a moment. Can you imagine walking with Jesus daily for three years, seeing his miracles, sitting under his teaching, hearing his voice, beholding his face, being in his presence, and then hearing him say, *Guys, trust me. I know you're sad right now. But it is going to be **even***

better *for you* **after** *I've gone away?* I'm sure the faces of the disciples looked more than a little sceptical (especially that Thomas guy).

Jesus was going to go away. He would be crucified and raised from the dead, and would ascend to the Father. And according to Jesus, not only would his departure *not* be a loss to the mission he was sending them into the world for; it would actually be a *gain*. How can that be? To use a sporting metaphor, how on earth is it possible that the absence of the team captain (who is also the greatest player to ever live) proves to be better for his team-mates?

Because he would send them the Holy Spirit.

> *"Nevertheless, I tell you the truth: it is to your advantage that I go away, for if I do not go away, the Helper will not come to you. But if I go, I will send him to you."*

The Holy Spirit would be a better teacher than Jesus, not because he would teach the disciples a new or superior doctrine, but because he is the one who opens our eyes to truly understand Jesus' words. "He will glorify me, for he will take what is mine and declare it to you" (v 14).

The Holy Spirit is a better comforter than Jesus, not because the Spirit cares more for you than Jesus does but because he dwells *within* you—24 hours a day, seven days a week. Think about that: the same Holy Spirit who powerfully raised Christ from the dead is the very one whom Jesus has sent to live in you (Romans 8:11). Unlike Jesus during his time on earth, the Spirit does not sleep or rest. He is not confined to one conversation in one place at a time. He is the Helper to every single one of God's people, every day, and he's never going to leave them.

Consider a small sample of the thousands of ways that God the Holy Spirit is at work in your life right now:

- When you were dead in your sins, it was the Spirit who cracked open your heart to Jesus (Titus 3:5-6).

- When you don't know what to do, it is the Holy Spirit who guides you, convicts you of sin, and gives you the wisdom you need (John 16:13).

- When you don't understand God's word, it is the Holy Spirit who illuminates your understanding and points you to Jesus (Psalm 119:18; John 14:26).

- When you're not sure if you have any right to approach God, it is the Spirit who reminds you that you can now approach God as *Father* (Galatians 4:6).

- When you're intimidated by the world and tempted to shut up about Jesus, it is the Spirit who fills you with power to hold fast to the gospel and keep boldly telling the good news to anyone who will listen (Acts 4:31).

- When you're going through a time that requires great endurance, it is the Spirit who gives you assurance by pouring afresh the blazing, life-renewing love of the triune God into your heart (Romans 5:5).

- When you don't know what to pray and your prayers are reduced to little more than groans and sighs directed towards God, it is the Holy Spirit who "intercedes for us ... according to the will of God" (Romans 8:26-27), discerning the prayer within our groaning, and "[fixing] our prayers on the way up".[21]

Is it any wonder that Jesus said, *It is to your advantage that I go away, so that the Helper may come*? The implication is that if Jesus *didn't* go, the Spirit *wouldn't* be sent to us. And to

---

21 J.I. Packer and Carolyn Nystrom, *Praying: Finding Our Way Through Duty to Delight* (Intervarsity Press, 2006), p 175.

borrow J.D. Greear's wonderful phrase, Jesus knew that the Spirit's presence inside his followers would be incomparably better than his presence beside them.[22]

REFLECT
Take a few moments to marvel at God the Holy Spirit. Thank him for how he is currently at work in your life. Which of his works from the list above is most precious to you right now?

"Beloved, we can now see Jesus every hour, and every moment of every hour! So often as you bow the knee, His Spirit, who represents Him, can commune with you, and bless you. No matter whether it is in the dead of night that your cry goes up, or under the blaze of burning noon— there is the Spirit waiting to be gracious, and your sighs and cries climb up to Christ in heaven, and return with answers of peace! These difficulties did not occur to you, perhaps, in your first thoughts; but if you meditate awhile, you will see that the presence of the Spirit, avoiding that difficulty, makes Christ accessible to every saint at all times; not to a few choice favourites, but to every believing man and woman the Holy Spirit is accessible, and thus the whole body of the faithful can enjoy present and perpetual communion with Christ!"

Charles Spurgeon, "The Superlative Excellence of the Holy Spirit", Sermon #574

---

22 J.D. Greear, *Jesus Continued: Why the Spirit inside You is Better than Jesus beside You* (Zondervan, 2014), p 13.

CHAPTER 30

"Your sorrow will turn into joy"

READ JOHN 16:20-22

*M*ost of us have had something taken from us against our will or stolen from our possession. Once, when I was a teenager, I decided to sleep in and skip church. That morning, someone stole my car from our driveway. Needless to say, it was a long time before I skipped church again without a good reason! In these verses, Jesus promises his disciples a gift of joy that no one will ever be able ultimately to take away from them.

Knowing what lies ahead, Jesus gives his disciples a warning and a promise. He wants them to know that great sorrow lies ahead of them; specifically during his crucifixion but also generally through their lives this side of glory. Yet he also gives them a wonderful promise: "Your sorrow will turn into joy" (John 16:20). Two dimensions of joy are in view: the specific yet unspeakable joy that will flood their downcast hearts on Resurrection morning as Mary rushes in and announces, "I have seen the Lord!" (20:18); and also, more generally, the joy of living in light of Jesus' resurrection, even as they await the promise of his return.

To illustrate this pattern of sorrow and joy, Jesus speaks of a woman giving birth, saying that she "has sorrow because her hour has come, but when she has delivered the baby, she no longer remembers the anguish, for joy that a human being has been born into the world" (John 16:21). Joy and sorrow will both be realities for his followers in this lifetime, often in close proximity to each other.

But consider the example Jesus uses here at an even more basic level. When a mother meets her newborn child for the very first time and cradles close this incomparably precious gift, she forgets her pain. But that doesn't mean that her pain was not real. On the contrary, the greatness of her joy rises *out of* her sorrow—it does not bypass it. Yet neither does the sorrow overshadow her joy; that joy is something that no one can take away.

And so it is with us. Jesus promises you what he promised his first disciples:

"No one will take your joy from you." (v 22)

In Christ, we have a foretaste of such invincible joy now, as well as the certainty that its fullness is on the way. So what can possibly steal your joy, if your joy is grounded in the life, death and resurrection of Jesus?

Changing circumstances cannot steal your joy because, unlike the rest of the world, your ultimate hope is not in what is happening around you but in who Jesus is for you (Philippians 4:11-13).

Trials cannot steal your joy for, in Christ's hands, they have become your personal servants, preparing you for "an eternal weight of glory beyond all comparison" (2 Corinthians 4:17).

Betrayal cannot steal your joy for, even though every person in the world should desert you, Jesus never will (Hebrews 13:5-6).

Satan cannot steal your joy for Jesus has put him to shame and triumphed over him on your behalf (Colossians 2:15).

The best he can do now is lie to you, trying to convince you to go looking for joy somewhere other than Jesus. But he cannot ultimately take it away from you.

Sin cannot steal your joy for, in Christ's atoning death, you have received not only the gift of forgiveness for all your sins but the gift of repentance, which is itself a grace (2 Timothy 2:25). Is it any wonder that our hearts need to hear the gospel daily, so we can turn from sin and continually "rejoice in the Lord" (Philippians 4:4)?

Even death cannot steal your joy for Jesus has defeated death through his resurrection. To die is to be with the one in whose "presence there is fullness of joy" (Psalm 16:11). Nothing can take your joy from you, because nothing in all of creation can take Jesus from you (Romans 8:39). Have you ever considered that there is a day on God's calendar when someone's eye will leak out the very last recorded teardrop in human history (Revelation 21:4)? And then Jesus will catch that final tear with his finger and announce, *Ok, that's it. No more death, no more mourning, no more pain, no more loss. From here on out, it's only joy.* That day is most assuredly in our future. Until that day comes, hold fast to his promise:

> *"You have sorrow now, but I will see you again, and your hearts will rejoice, and no one will take your joy from you." (John 16:22)*

PRAY

Jesus, you are a great Saviour. Everything that grieves me right now I bring to you and entrust it to your hands because I am confident that you will turn every one of those sorrows into joy. Thank you for your resurrection. Thank you that this world is not how it will always be. Thank you that you are coming back, just as you promised. Deepen my joy in you today, and every day after it, until you bring me home into the eternal joy of being with you.

"Our sorrows are fish that come to us with money in their mouths. Whenever they come, they always bring us joy ... Is not that a wonderful promise? 'Your sorrow shall be turned into joy.' If any man here were greatly in debt and someone were to say, 'All your debts shall be transformed into assets,' well, it is clear that then the richest man here would be the man that had the biggest debts. So is it with our sorrows—the more of them that we have, the more joys we shall have, because they are to be turned into joy. If, as believers, we have much sorrow, we shall have much joy coming out of it, wherefore, with the apostle, 'we glory in tribulations also,' and triumph in the afflictions and trials of this mortal life, seeing that they shall work our lasting good."

Charles Spurgeon, "Joy in Place of Sorrow", Sermon #2525

CHAPTER 31

"Take heart; I have overcome the world"

READ JOHN 16:29-33

*E*very Christian is living simultaneously in two locations: first, in the world around them that is ever changing and ever raging; second, in the permanent love of Christ, who "is the same yesterday and today and forever" (Hebrews 13:8). In the first location (the world), Jesus promises us tribulation—a word that quite literally means "pressure". Doesn't that accurately describe a large part of life as followers of Jesus this side of glory—pressure? So we shouldn't be surprised when we find our commitment to Jesus being pressed in upon by our tri-fold enemy of the world, the flesh and the devil.

And yet Jesus also promises that as we follow him through the pressures of life in this world, we will do so as those who live in a second and superior reality: in him. And in him, he gives us an otherworldly peace that captures the attention of this world. In this way, the Christian can be in the midst of a great storm—figuratively or literally—and at the same time be enveloped by a peace that comes from knowing who rules the weather.

In Acts 3, Peter preaches a sermon that calls people to repent and turn to God so "that times of refreshing may come from the presence of the Lord" (Acts 3:20). That word "refreshing" in the Greek is *anapsyxis* which means "cooling, relief, a recovery of breath". Like a cold drink at the end of a hot day's work in the sun. Like the moment of coming up for air after holding your breath underwater. In the presence of Jesus, our life is depressurised. We can breathe again because, no matter what is happening around us, we are with Christ, whose peace surpasses understanding and stands guard over our hearts and minds (Philippians 4:7).

And because of this, Jesus says, *"Take heart; I have overcome the world"* (John 16:33). No matter what we're facing, we are always facing it from the position of "in Christ". To the degree that we settle this truth in our hearts, we will never be afraid again. When John Chrysostom was summoned before the Empress Eudoxia in the early years of the 5th century, because he would not bend to the pressures of her politics, she threatened him with banishment. Chrysostom responded:

> *"'You cannot banish me, for this world is my Father's house.'*
>
> *'Then I will kill you,' said the empress.*
>
> *'No, you cannot, for my life is hid with Christ in God,' Chrysostom responded.*
>
> *'Then I will take away your treasures,' said she.*
>
> *'No, you cannot, for my treasure is in heaven, and my heart is there,' Chrysostom replied.*
>
> *'Then I will drive you away from your friends and you will have no one left,' she challenged a final time. And Chrysostom, knowing the supernatural peace that Christ alone gives his people in the midst of their earthly tribulations, said to her, 'No, you cannot, for I have a*

friend in heaven from whom you cannot separate me. I
defy you, for there is nothing you can do to harm me.'" [23]

Today you are in this world, surrounded by its pressures. And one day, that will change.

Today you are in Christ, enveloped by his peace. And that will never change.

Your union with him goes deeper than just him being with you. You are *in him*, which means you will share not only in his sufferings but in his resurrection. His future is now your future. His triumph over sin has been gifted to you. In Jesus, and only in Jesus and always in Jesus, is peace of the truest and trustiest and most enduring kind. In him you have a shelter for every storm, a compass for every confusion and omnipotent strength for every tribulation. In him, though you still have a journey to walk, you are already home.

"I have said these things to you, that in me you may have
peace. In the world you will have tribulation. But take
heart; I have overcome the world." (John 16:33)

PRAY

Pray Psalm 27:1-6 out loud: "The LORD is my light and my salvation; whom shall I fear? The LORD is the stronghold of my life; of whom shall I be afraid? When evildoers assail me to eat up my flesh, my adversaries and foes, it is they who stumble and fall. Though an army encamp against me, my heart shall not fear; though war arise against me, yet I will be confident. One thing have I asked of the LORD, that will I seek after: that I may dwell in the house of the LORD all the days of my life, to gaze upon the beauty of the LORD and to enquire in his temple. For he will hide me in his shelter in the day of trouble; he will conceal me under the cover of his

---

23 R. Kent Hughes, *Romans: Righteousness from Heaven* (Crossway, 1991), p 171.

tent; he will lift me high upon a rock. And now my head shall be lifted up above my enemies all around me, and I will offer in his tent sacrifices with shouts of joy; I will sing and make melody to the LORD."

"So, brothers and sisters, let us go back to the world and its tribulations without fear! Its trials cannot hurt us! In the process we shall get good, as the wheat does out of the threshing. Let us go forth to combat the world, for it cannot overcome us! There was never a man, yet, with the life of God in his soul, whom the whole world could subdue! No, all the world and hell together cannot conquer the smallest baby in the family of the Lord Jesus Christ! Lo, you are harnessed with salvation! You are covered with omnipotence! Your heads are covered with the protection of the atonement, and Christ, Himself, the Son of God, is your captain! Take up your battle cry with courage and fear not, for more is He that is for you than all they that are against you! It is said of the glorified saints, 'They overcame through the blood of the Lamb'; 'and this is the victory which overcomes the world, even our faith.' Be steadfast even to the end, for you shall be more than conquerors through Him that has loved you."

Charles Spurgeon, "Christ the Overcomer of the World", Sermon #1327

CHAPTER 32

"Father, the hour has come; glorify your Son"

READ JOHN 17:1-5

Can you imagine what it would be like to hear Jesus praying for you? As Jesus finishes his final instructions to the disciples in John 16 with the encouragement, "Take heart; I have overcome the world" (John 16:33), he turns his face upward and begins to pray. And what follows in John 17 is one of the most sacred moments recorded in all of Scripture—Jesus interceding for his people. This is holy ground. The great High Priest is pouring out his heart, to the Father, for us.

What does it do in your heart to know that Jesus, on his final evening, thought of you and brought you before the Father in prayer? And what if I told you that he continues to pray for you now? Hebrews 7:25 tells us that "he is able to save to the uttermost those who draw near to God through him, since he always lives to make intercession for them". To intercede means to stand in the gap on behalf of another. That's what Jesus did on his final night. That's what Jesus did on the cross. That's what Jesus is doing for you now. It's one of the most astonishing facts of the gospel: that Christ's prayer for you in John 17 is merely a preview of his present ministry on your behalf at this very moment. So let me ask you again: how might you face this coming day if you were convinced that Jesus has your name on his lips in the throne room of God, right now? The Scottish preacher Robert Murray M'Cheyne wrote, "If I could hear Christ praying for me in the next room, I would not fear a million enemies. Yet distance makes no difference. He is praying for me."[24]

And we can be sure of this: any prayer that Jesus has prayed on our behalf, the Father rejoices in answering. Which means that when Jesus said that he has authority "to give eternal life to all whom [the Father has] given him" (John 17:2), he was not making your salvation a possibility that you might take advantage of. Your salvation was a certainty. So much so that Jesus treasures each and every one of us as a gift to him from the Father: one that he delights over. When Jesus declared that he had completed the work the Father gave him to do (v 4), it meant that everything required to secure your place in God's family has been done. When Jesus prayed, "Father, glorify me in your own presence with the glory that I had with you before the world existed" (v 5), there was zero doubt that the Father would do exactly that. And Jesus would walk through the crucifixion, into a resurrection, and ascend back to his rightful throne as "the King of the ages ... the only God, [who is worthy of] honour and glory for ever and ever" (1 Timothy 1:17).

And here, in John 17, it begins. The hour was upon him (John 17:1): the hour he had come for. The hour that his whole earthly life had been unmistakably moving towards. The hour when, after being bruised, beaten, spat upon, shamed, and lacerated with a Roman whip, his mangled body

---

24 Andrew Bonar, *Memoir and Remains of the Rev. Robert Murray M'Cheyne* (Oliphant, Anderson, & Ferrier, 1883), p 158.

would be lifted high and nailed to a couple of pieces of wood. The cross would be the altar upon which, as John the Baptiser prophesied, Jesus would be "the Lamb of God, who takes away the sin of the world" (John 1:29). And Jesus prayed that this hour—the hour of man's greatest evil and Christ's greatest humiliation—would be the hour of his glory. His hour had come, and he knew it. So he prayed:

> *"Father, the hour has come; glorify your Son that the Son may glorify you." (John 17:1)*

So great was our Saviour's humility that even his prayer to be glorified in the hour of his passion was so that his glory would bring glory to the Father. And while Jesus alone has the divine right to pray that the Father would glorify him, he yet leaves us a model for our own prayers: "God, be glorified in me". Is there anywhere in your life right now where, deep down, you're longing not for God's glory to be revealed but your own? Surrender that area to him now and rest in the better prayers of Jesus on your behalf, that you may know him and life eternal in him. It is what he is praying for you even now.

REFLECT
Read the whole of John 17. Take a few moments to really listen to what Jesus prays for you. Then respond to him— not with any requests right now but simply in gratitude and worship for the Saviour that he is.

> *"In the face of Jesus, who is the express image of the Father, God is glorified to the full. In the death of Christ, above all things, God is glorified, for there all the attributes of God are seen. There was the power which sustained*

*Christ beneath his more than Herculean task; the love
which surrendered the darling of its bosom that he might
die instead of traitors; the justice which would not, could
not, forgive sin without satisfaction; the truth which had
threatened to punish, and did punish; which had promised
to give a Saviour, and did give him; the faithfulness to the
covenant which kept that covenant at such a dread expense;
the wisdom which planned the marvellous way of salvation
by a substitute. Nay, let me put it all together: the wholeness,
the holiness of God, yea, all his attributes are seen, each
one equally magnified in the death of Jesus Christ. He is
glorious, and the triune God is glorified in him."*

Charles Spurgeon, "The Son Glorified by the Father and the
Father Glorified by the Son", Sermon #1465A

CHAPTER 33

"Sanctify them in the truth"

READ JOHN 17:15-19

John 17 is a stunning behind-the-curtain look into the prayer life of Jesus. It is said that John Knox, the Scottish Reformer, had this chapter read to him every single day in the final days of his life. Another theologian said that it is "without doubt, the most remarkable portion of the most remarkable book in the world".[25] Among the many requests that Jesus makes on our behalf to the Father in this portion of Scripture, we hear him pray the following:

> *"Sanctify them in the truth; your word is truth."*
>
> *(John 17:17)*

Jesus is praying for the Twelve here, but he widens his prayer to include all believers in verse 20. To sanctify is "to set apart". Jesus is not praying that his people would isolate themselves from the world as a community of recluses (see v 15), but that they would possess a visible distinctiveness in the midst of the world that reveals they belong to Jesus. Paul reminds us that when we face life without the grumbling and argumentativeness that mars so much of our era, we

---

25 Arthur W. Pink, *Exposition of the Gospel of John: Volume Three – John 15:7 to end* (Zondervan, 1974), p 90.

demonstrate ourselves to be "children of God who are faultless in a crooked and perverted generation, among whom you shine like stars in the world, by holding firm to the word of life" (Philippians 2:15-16, CSB).

"Sanctify them in the truth; your word is truth."

According to Jesus, what sets us apart is the way God's word gives shape to our lives. I have found that time and time again, my walk with Jesus rises and falls with my reading of the Scriptures. It's not that his love for me fluctuates when I spend less time in his word. Not at all! It's that my love for him does. When a husband and wife stop communicating with and listening to one another, their love fades accordingly. In the same way, apathy towards God's word leads to lovelessness—and, eventually, apathy in our witness.

"Sanctify them in the truth; your word is truth. As you sent me into the world, so I have sent them into the world."

You see, your sanctification goes far deeper than a private pursuit of personal holiness. Your sanctification is part of Christ's mission for the world! The world takes no notice of those who mirror back to them their own patterns of thinking, living, and pursuing. But they will notice someone who reminds them of Jesus. Even if they know nothing of the real Jesus, the set-apartness of Christians becomes a living sermon to them of the truth.

"Sanctify them in the truth; your word is truth."

God's word is both a mirror and a window. It is a mirror in that it shows us ourselves as we truly are. Yet it is also a window that we look through to see Christ, and our true and glorious future in him. The gap between what we see in the mirror and what we behold through the window is the gap of sanctification. And the Christian life is one of looking and re-looking to Jesus through the window of God's word, and being gradually formed into his likeness by the power of the Holy Spirit (2 Corinthians 3:18).

"Sanctify them in the truth."

In this way, the lifelong process of sanctification is really that of *congruence*, in which our lives are daily yet definitely being brought in line with our profession. Eugene Peterson writes, "The Christian life is the lifelong practice of attending to the details of congruence—congruence between ends and means, congruence between what we do and the way we do it, congruence between what is written in Scripture and our living out what is written ... the congruence of the Word made flesh in Jesus with what is lived in our flesh."[26]

If God's word is the means of our sanctification, is there a greater priority in our day than making space to hear from him? We all have a long way to go, but here's something I can state with 100% confidence: if you give yourself to patient, relational, intentional Bible-reading that learns to behold Jesus throughout all of Scripture, you will become a congruent Christian, your life validating your lips, and you will be living proof in this world of the power of God.

It is what Jesus prays for you. And God the Father promises to answer his prayer for you. He will indeed complete the work he has begun in your life (Philippians 1:6). He will indeed set you apart. He will indeed close the gap throughout your life. And on the day he calls you home, and your face beholds the glory of God in the face of your Saviour, you will reflect him. You will be fully sanctified. You will be whole. And the glory of the Lord Jesus will be reflected perfectly in you (Romans 8:17).

---

26 John Brown quoted in Eugene H. Peterson, *As Kingfishers Catch Fire: A Conversation on the Ways of God Formed by the Words of God* (Waterbrook, 2017), p xviii.

PRAY

Jesus, thank you for praying for me. Thank you that your commitment to completing the work you have begun in me is infinitely greater than my commitment to you. I confess that I can't change myself. Only you can do that. So change me, Lord. Make me more like you today. Show me in your word the ways in which I need you. And then show me yourself.

> *"We are not the world's, else might we be ambitious; we are not Satan's, else might we be covetous; we are not our own, else might we be selfish. We are bought with a price, and hence we are His by whom the price is paid. We belong to Jesus, and He presents us to His Father, and begs Him to accept us and sanctify us to His own purposes. Do we not most heartily concur in this dedication? Do we not cry, 'Father, sanctify us to Your service?' I am sure we do if we have realised our redeemed condition ... This is our prayer: Lord, spiritualise us, elevate us, make us to dwell in communion with God, make us to know Him whom flesh and blood cannot reveal or discern. May the Spirit of the living God have full sovereignty over us and perfect in us the will of the Lord, for this is to be sanctified."*

Charles Spurgeon, "Our Lord's Prayer for His People's Sanctification", Sermon #1890

CHAPTER 34

"That they may be one"

READ JOHN 17:20-23

*T*he oneness of his people matters to Jesus. So oneness must matter to us. In fact, so important is it to him that he asks the Father four times in his John 17 prayer that we may be one *to the same degree* that Jesus and the Father are one (v 11, 21, 22, 23). Such a supernatural unity not only reflects something of the beauty of the triune God in his people; it also reveals that beauty to the world. And in this way, genuine Christian unity is another one of God's methods of saving people to himself.

> *"May [they] all be one ... so that the world may believe that you have sent me." (v 21)*

Jesus has already said as much to the disciples. After washing their feet, he told them that the world would know that they are his disciples by their love for one another (John 13:35). And here, what he has commanded of his people, he requests of his Father in heartfelt prayer. According to Jesus, the credibility of our witness will be undergirded by the reality of our oneness. So much so, Francis Schaeffer says, that Jesus' words in John 17:21 should sober us because, through this prayer, "Jesus gives the world the right to judge whether the

Father has sent the Son on the basis of whether the world sees observable love among all true Christians."[27]

In a world divided in a thousand different ways, unity in the church becomes a captivating witness to the reality of God's love in Jesus Christ (v 23). Our togetherness becomes a living and non-ignorable sermon. The surprising reality of our unity validates the surprising truth of the gospel, since love like ours could only be supernatural. The church is living proof of Jesus' power to change people. Is it any wonder, then, that Jesus would repeatedly pray for our unity?

Here we must pause and remember two important truths about the unity Jesus prays for. First, we should be careful not to mistake oneness for sameness. That's not the beautiful unity described by Jesus, but the suffocating straitjacket of uniformity. Rather, true unity is the Spirit-powered generosity of God's people towards one another in the midst of their diversity, for the sake of Christ, that the world will find compelling.

Second, we will never know true unity with other Christians by seeking unity directly. If we aim at unity for the sake of unity, we will only ever end up with a watered-down ecumenical compromise that is impotent for any real impact in the world around us. No, unity is not the goal. Unity is the by-product. A.W. Tozer writes:

> "Has it ever occurred to you that one hundred pianos all tuned to the same fork are automatically tuned to each other? They are of one accord by being tuned, not to each other, but to another standard to which each one must individually bow. So one hundred worshipers met together, each one looking away to Christ, are in heart nearer to each other than they could possibly be were they to become 'unity'

---

27 Francis Schaeffer, *The Church Before the Watching World* (Crossway Books, 1985), p 143.

conscious and turn their eyes away from God to strive for closer fellowship."[28]

The only way to experience true oneness with one another is by making Jesus—the real Jesus—our goal. And when we do, not only will the world see that he is who he claimed to be and has accomplished what the Father sent him to do but also that the Father has loved us with the same love with which he loves Jesus.

> *"I am in them and you are in me, so that they may be made completely one, that the world may know you have sent me and have loved them as you have loved me."*
>
> *(v 23, CSB)*

Don't hurry past this. Press these precious words into your heart. God the Father loves you with the same nuclear intensity that he loves the Son. Now we see why Paul prayed that we "may have strength to comprehend with all the saints what is the breadth and length and height and depth, and to know the love of Christ that surpasses knowledge" (Ephesians 3:18-19). We need divine strength just to comprehend the vastness of God's love for us in Christ! And Jesus prays this out loud in front of his followers so that they know it and become convinced of it.

It's what he prays for you too.

PRAY

Personalise the following prayer drawn from Ephesians 3:16-19 and 4:1-3: "Father, according to the riches of your glory, strengthen me today with power in my inner being through your Holy Spirit, so that Christ may dwell in my heart through faith. Ground me in your love with deep roots, so that I can begin to grasp with all the saints what

---

28 A.W. Tozer, *The Pursuit of God* (Authentic Media, 2004), p 88-89.

is the length and width and height and depth of your love, and to know the love of Christ surpasses knowledge. Fill me with your fullness, O God. Help me to live worthy of such love, through humility, gentleness, and patience with other Christians: to bear with them in love, as you have done with me, and to eagerly maintain the unity of the Spirit, whom you have given to all your people. Amen."

"It is significant, beloved, that the Saviour should in His last moments not only desire the salvation of all His people, but should plead for the unity of the saved ones, that being saved they might be united. It was not enough that each sheep should be taken from the jaw of the wolf, He would have all the sheep gathered into one fold under His own care ... Christ's prayer for His people is the great motive force by which the Spirit of God is sent to us, and the whole church is kept filled with life, and the whole of that force is tending to this one thing—to unity. It is removing everything which keeps us from being one. It is working with all its divine omnipotence to bring us into a visible unity when Christ shall stand in the latter days upon the earth. Beloved, let us have hope for sinners yet unconverted; Christ is praying for them. Let us have hope for the entire body of the faithful; Christ is praying for their unity, and what He prays for must be effected, [for] He never pleads in vain."

Charles Spurgeon, "Unity in Christ", Sermon #668

CHAPTER 35

"Shall I not drink the cup?"

READ JOHN 18:1-11

*T*n a garden, on a dark night, on the cusp of the most important event that all of history had been building toward, Peter missed.

Twice.

First, he missed with Malchus, and Malchus lost an ear. At the risk of overstating the obvious, Peter was not aiming his blade at this man's ear, as if he were making some kind of well-aimed surgical strike. He was trying to take that man's head off! Fortunately for Malchus, he missed. Yet even here, Luke tells us—as Jesus is betrayed—the compassion of Jesus is put on display as he enters into the pain of this stranger, miraculously healing the wound Peter had inflicted (Luke 22:51).

Second, and more importantly, Peter had missed the point of everything that evening that Jesus had been teaching his disciples; the hour for which Jesus had come into the world had arrived (John 12:27). Jesus was born to die so that his people would live forever. And so he turns to Peter and says:

"Put your sword into its sheath; shall I not drink the cup that the Father has given me?" (John 18:11)

Had Jesus wanted physical defence, he would have provided his own. And with ease. After all, the one who commands storms, walks on waves and orders around demons has little need of a dagger in the hands of a fisherman. In fact, moments earlier Jesus had flexed his divine power and with three simple words knocked the entire contingent of soldiers off their feet and onto the ground (v 6). Yet the final words that Jesus would say that night to Peter—one of his most loyal, yet most impulsive, disciples—remind us that nothing ranked higher to Jesus than accomplishing the work his Father had given him.

Peter, are you really going to stand between me, and the cup I have come into this world to drink?

You see, something important had taken place before the arrival of Judas and the soldiers in verse 2. The other Gospel accounts fill in the details. Under such great stress that the capillaries within his sweat glands burst so that he was literally perspiring blood, Jesus prayed, "My Father, if it be possible, let this cup pass from me; nevertheless, not as I will, but as you will" (Matthew 26:39). It was here that Jesus settled it in his heart to drink the cup of God's righteous wrath that our sin earned. He would drink every last drop of divine judgment. As he laid down his life, he would drain the cup dry. Why? So that you and I would never have to. This is why he had come into the world: as the second Adam, to redeem us from the curse of the first Adam. And the only way he could do that was by taking that curse of our sin onto himself (Galatians 3:13).

Tim Keller was the first to help me see the prophetic symbolism and parallels between Adam in the Garden of Eden and Jesus—the second Adam—in the Garden of Gethsemane.[29]

---

29 Timothy Keller, *Encounters with Jesus: Unexpected Answers to Life's Biggest Questions* (Hodder & Stoughton, 2013), p 163-164.

In the first garden, faced with the choice to obey or disobey God about the tree, Adam disobeyed. His sin essentially declared, *Father, not your will, but mine be done.* In the second garden, faced with the choice to obey or disobey God about the tree—a different tree (the cross)—Jesus obeyed. "He himself bore our sins in his body on the tree" (1 Peter 2:24). And as he stared into the looming cup of divine judgement that was rightfully ours to drink, he prayed to his Father, "Not my will, but yours, be done" (Luke 22:42). What Adam lost in Eden, Jesus won back in Gethsemane and secured at Calvary. As Paul declares in Romans 5:19, "For as by the one man's disobedience the many were made sinners, so by the one man's obedience the many will be made righteous."

"Shall I not drink the cup that the Father has given me?"

You see, the passion of Jesus did not begin when he bled on the cross. It began when he bled in the garden and resolved that he would indeed drink the cup of condemnation—our cup of condemnation. And because he did that, "there is therefore now no condemnation for those who are in Christ Jesus" (Romans 8:1).

PRAY
Lord, it is hard for me to believe the lengths you went to for the sake of my sin. Thank you for drinking the cup that belonged to me. Words fail me; help me never again doubt the greatness of your love for me. And teach me to say with you, through my own little Gethsemanes along the way, "Father, not my will, but your will be done".

"May we not conceive that, as in a garden Adam's self-indulgence ruined us, so in another garden the agonies of

*the Second Adam should restore us? Gethsemane supplies the medicine for the ills which followed upon the forbidden fruit of Eden! ... Brothers and sisters, that was no trifling suffering which made recompense to the justice of God for the sins of men! I am never afraid of exaggeration when I speak of what my Lord endured. All hell was distilled into that cup of which our God and Saviour, Jesus Christ, was made to drink! ... He had not yet come to the raging billows of the penalty, itself, but even standing on the shore, as He heard the awful surf breaking at His feet, His soul was sorely amazed and very heavy! It was the shadow of the coming tempest; it was the prelude of the dread desertion which He had to endure when **He** stood where **we** ought to have stood, and paid to His Father's justice the debt which was due from us!"*

Charles Spurgeon, "The Agony in Gethsemane", Sermon #1199

CHAPTER 36

"My kingdom is not of this world"

READ JOHN 18:33-38

"*A*re *you* the King of the Jews?" (John 18:33, my emphasis.) We can almost hear the disbelief in Pilate's voice. At this point, Jesus didn't look very much like a king. He was beaten, sleep-deprived, bruised and bleeding, with the worst still ahead of him. Having been arrested, questioned and accused of blasphemy by Caiaphas the high priest and the religious leaders, Jesus was brought before Pilate. Had the Jewish leaders just wanted to punish Jesus, they could have done so. But they didn't want to merely punish Jesus; they wanted to kill him— and shame him in the process. They wanted crucifixion. And a governor's permission was required for that.

The interrogation begins: *"Are you the King of the Jews?"* (v 33).

After a brief volley of questions, Jesus answers Pilate, "My kingdom is not of this world" (v 36). He is indeed a king. But his ambitions aren't manifest through political power plays or military might. If they were, he reminds Pilate, "my servants would have been fighting". More than that, at any moment, Jesus, the King of heaven, could have summoned legions of angels to appear in glory so blazing and so bright that the mere sight of them would have brought the entire Roman Empire to its knees.

> *"My kingdom is not of this world ... For this purpose I have come into the world—to bear witness to the truth. Everyone who is of the truth listens to my voice." (v 36-37)*

In Jesus, the kingdom of God, promised throughout the Old Testament, had broken into this world. When Jesus began his public ministry, he preached, "The time is fulfilled, and the kingdom of God is at hand; repent and believe in the gospel" (Mark 1:15). What did he mean by that? The kingdom of God had come near because the King of the kingdom was near. In fact, he was standing right in front of his hearers. And his kingdom would not look like earthly kingdoms. Earthly kings glory in their strength, but Jesus' glory was his sacrifice. Earthly kings hold on to their rights and privileges and comforts. Jesus laid his down. His is a kingdom where the first are last and the last are first, where it's better to give than receive, and where greatness is measured by serving rather than being served because Jesus is the kind of king who leads by example. And he inaugurated his kingdom by leaving his heavenly throne and being born in a barn, by making himself last, by giving himself away, by bending low to serve and by dying for his enemies. Can you see how the kingdom of Jesus is "not of this world"?

Jesus came to reveal what is true about God and us and the future of this world. Like light breaking into a dark room through a crack in the door, Christ came like a dazzling sunbeam of truth into a world covered in the darkness of sin. His kingdom is advanced not by might but by a message. A message that God is true to his promises. A message that the true King has come, bringing pardon and amnesty to a world in rebellion against him, for all who will receive him. A message that the violence and deception and exploitation that mark the earthly kingdoms of this age are not how it's always going to be.

The kingdom of Jesus has come near. It has begun. And if you love him, you have been swept up into it because you have heard what Pilate did not hear—the truth of Christ's voice. The moment his voice opened your heart to believe, you became a citizen of heaven (Philippians 3:20) and an ambassador of heaven's King (2 Corinthians 5:20). You have been entrusted with the same message of truth and ministry of reconciliation that Jesus came into this world to announce. His kingdom is, right now, breaking in through you and through all of his people. And one day soon, the King will return, and the prayer he taught his followers will be prophetically fulfilled by him, whose "kingdom [will have] come ... on earth as it is in heaven" (Matthew 6:10).

As it turns out, here in John 18, both Pilate and the sub-heading on that page in your Bible are wrong. (Don't fret: that part is not *Spirit-inspired!*) This passage is not *really* about "Jesus before Pilate". That's not how Jesus viewed this encounter. What all of heaven saw was *Pilate before Jesus*. The man before his Maker; the created one before the Creator; the clay before the Potter; the governor of Judea before the King of glory.

PRAY

Lord Jesus, I remind myself today that you—and you alone—are the one who is in charge. Not only of my life but the entire universe. And because you are in control, I can stop pretending to be. Today I come again to your throne of grace, trusting you for the help and mercy that you alone can give. Your word is my treasure, your sovereignty is my sanity, your glory is my delight. Help me to live as a citizen of your kingdom today as I seek to serve others. Amen.

"Our Lord's claim to be a king shall be acknowledged one day by all mankind. When Christ said to Pilate, according to our version, 'You say that I am a king,' He virtually prophesied the future confession of all men. Some, taught by His grace, shall in this life rejoice in Him as their altogether lovely King. Blessed be God, the Lord Jesus might look into the eyes of many of us and say, 'You say that I am a king,' and we would reply, 'We do say it joyfully.' But the day shall come when He shall sit upon His great white throne, and then, when the multitudes shall tremble in the presence of His awful majesty, even such as Pontius Pilate, and Herod, and the chief priests shall own that He is a King! Then to each of His astounded and overwhelmingly convinced enemies He might say, 'Now, O despiser, you say that I am a King,' for to Him every knee shall bow, and every tongue shall confess that He is Lord!"

Charles Spurgeon, "Jesus, the King of Truth", Sermon #1086

CHAPTER 37

"Behold, your son! Behold, your mother!"

READ JOHN 19:16-18, 25-27

*H*ow many times, while he was just a baby, did the infant Jesus catch a glimpse of his mother and reach out his arms for her to hold him? How many times, while he was a little boy, did Mary open her arms wide to him after he had fallen and scraped his knees, sweeping him up into an embrace of motherly affection? As I did with my own children when they were little, I wonder if she ever playfully asked her young miracle-child, "How much do you love me?" And then laughed as he stretched his little arms as wide as they could go and said, "I love you thiiiiiiiss much!"

Clothed in blood and gasping for breath, Jesus looks down from the cross. And with his arms spread wide, his eyes meet those of his weeping mother. And there is no question about his love. The ancient prophecy that one born of woman would crush the head of the serpent (Genesis 3:15) was about to come true.

But so too was another. Simeon prophesied in Luke 2:35 that a sword would pierce Mary's soul. And here she feels the tip of its blade.

Yet in the midst of his own excruciating suffering, Jesus enters into his mother's suffering. Despite his own agony, Jesus gives thought to hers. And seeing John—"the disciple whom he loved" (John 19:26)—beside her, Jesus entrusts her wellbeing into the hands of his faithful friend.

> *"'Woman, behold, your son!'" Then he said to the disciple, 'Behold, your mother!'" (v 27)*

It seems likely from this that Joseph is no longer alive, and with Mary now about to lose her oldest son, "the disciple whom [Jesus] loved" is charged with a sacred responsibility: the care and protection of Jesus' own mother. Yet Jesus' words were more than just a demonstration of divine tenderness. They were indicative of a profound new spiritual reality that would take place under the cross.

You see, one of the most wonderful implications of the gospel is that we are not only saved *from* something but *to* something. Jesus saves us from sin. But he also saves us to himself. As our Saviour and our Lord, we belong to him (Romans 1:6). And while our salvation is deeply personal, it is never individual because to belong to Jesus means belonging to his family.

So now, we belong not only to Christ but to one another (1 Corinthians 12:15-20). There's a reason why the Christians of the 1st century (and every century since) rejoiced in calling one another "brothers and sisters". In fact, between Acts and Revelation, such language is used over 140 times. Older men and women in the faith are viewed as "fathers and mothers" (1 Timothy 5:1-2), and Paul addressed his letters to the younger Timothy and Titus with the affectionate phrase, "To … my true child in the faith" (1 Timothy 1:2; Titus 1:4).

As they stood at the foot of the cross, under the open arms of Jesus, those who were unrelated by blood were knit together through his blood. In the joining of his mother,

Mary, to John and John to her, Jesus gives us a preview of the eternal spiritual reality that the church embodies as the family of God. And John did not hesitate to obey: "From that hour [he] took her to his own home" (v 27). One historical account tells us that Mary lived in the home John owned for the next eleven years until her death. Another says she died in Ephesus, while joining John in his missionary work.[30] Whatever happened, we know that John took the responsibility given to him by his Saviour seriously.

Through his cross, Jesus makes us family. Family is who we open our arms wide to. To be family communicates that we are ever welcome, that we are loved and that we belong. And with the welcome that Jesus extended to us, we welcome in each other (Romans 15:7).

As you gather next with your church, look around you. Open your heart to them. Behold them and love them! And look for ways to meaningfully show them that you do. The family dynamics of God's people matter deeply to Jesus. So they matter deeply to us. Let's refuse to treat lightly that which Jesus gave his precious blood for: one another.

REFLECT

Take a few minutes to think about your spiritual family. As the Holy Spirit brings certain names and faces to mind, pray for them. Send them a message. Tell them you love them. Look for ways over this coming week to open your arms wide to them.

"What a family we shall be when we all rise together
and all the changed ones stand with us, all of one race,

---

30 R. Kent Hughes, *John: That You May Believe* (Crossway Books, 1999), p 446.

*all regenerate, all clothed in the white robe of Jesus'
righteousness! What a family! What a meeting it will be!
... Dear brothers and sisters, we shall live together in
heaven for ever. Let us love each other fervently, now, with
a pure heart. Help your poor brothers and sisters; cheer
your desponding brothers and sisters. Let no man look
only on his own things, but every man also on the things
of others. Brother, be brotherly. Sister, be a true sister. Let
us not love in word only, but in deed and in truth, for we
shall soon be at home together in our Father's house on
high."*

Charles Spurgeon, "Saints in Heaven and Earth One Family",
Sermon #1249

CHAPTER 38

"I thirst"

READ JOHN 19:23-24, 28-37

One of the most compelling witnesses that testifies to the Bible being a supernatural book, and Jesus being the promised one that history had been waiting for, is the fulfilment of prophecy. What was predicted throughout the Old Testament was embodied and revealed by Jesus in the New Testament. In fact, through his life, death and resurrection, Jesus fulfilled over 300 such prophecies. The probably of even just eight of these prophecies being perfectly satisfied by a single person is 1 in 100,000,000,000,000,000 (100 quadrillion).[31] And here, John wants to make sure that we see that Jesus is not of this world. So he zeroes in explicitly on four of them. He writes with one goal in mind: that you and I may know "that he is telling the truth—that you also may believe" (John 19:35).

First, there is the prophecy about the Saviour's clothes. Over 1,000 years earlier, David wrote in Psalm 22, "They have pierced my hands and feet" (v 16) and "they divide my garments among them, and for my clothing they cast lots" (v 18). And here, as Jesus slowly suffocates, with his hands

---

31 Peter W. Stoner and Robert C. Newman, *Science Speaks: Scientific Proof of the Accuracy of Prophecy and the Bible* (Moody, 1976), p 101-106.

and feet nailed to the cross, a group of soldiers divide up his clothes. In doing so, they unknowingly validate the identity of the Messiah dying above them.

A second prophecy from David fulfilled by Jesus comes from Psalm 34:19-20, which reads, "Many are the afflictions of the righteous, but the Lord delivers him out of them all. He keeps all his bones; not one of them is broken." Though the soldiers broke the legs of the two criminals being crucified next to Jesus, in order to speed up their deaths, they did not do so to Jesus. And John wants us to know that "these things took place that the Scripture might be fulfilled" (John 19:36).

A third prophecy was about how Jesus would be pierced. To ensure he really was dead, one of the soldiers "pierced his side with a spear, and at once there came out blood and water" (v 34). This was no coma or near-death experience; by this point, Jesus really was dead. And this was prophesied 500 years earlier by Zechariah. Actually, the whole book of Zechariah is about how the Saviour would come. Among other things, he even prophesied that the Messiah would enter Jerusalem riding on a donkey (Zechariah 9:9) and be betrayed for 30 pieces of silver (11:12-13). Yet here, John draws our attention to Zechariah 12:10: "They will look on him whom they have pierced".

Yet before Jesus passed away, one of the seven cries that escaped his lips on the cross was two simple words: "I thirst" (John 19:28). And as Jesus hung there—betrayed, mocked, disgraced and dying—one of the soldiers "put a sponge full of the sour wine on a hyssop branch and held it to his mouth" (v 29). Centuries earlier, David had pointed us towards this very moment when he wrote Psalm 69:19-21 (CSB):

"You know the insults I endure—my shame and disgrace. You are aware of all my adversaries. Insults have broken my heart, and I am in despair. I waited for sympathy, but

there was none; for comforters, but found no one. Instead,
they gave me gall for my food, and for my thirst they gave
me vinegar to drink."

Here we see both Christ's humanity and his deity. *"I thirst."*
What a juxtaposition! Deity cries aloud from parched lips.
He who spoke a word and turned water into wine; he who
said, "If anyone thirsts, let him come to me and drink" (John
7:37); he who drank the cup of damnation dry so that we
would never have to is yet thirsty.

"After this, Jesus, knowing that all was now finished, said
(to fulfil the Scripture), 'I thirst'." (v 28)

He does not speak a word of power to answer his own need.
He could have, you know. He had every right and ability to
flex his divinity and quench his thirst. But instead, here in
his final moments, he chooses to express the fullness of his
humanity. *"I thirst."* Why? Because he had come to "fulfil
the Scripture". Because he knew that "all was now finished".
Because he is our great High Priest, who can sympathise with
every weakness and need we will ever face in our humanity
(Hebrews 4:15), and he shows us what it looks like to entrust
them into the Father's hands.

PRAY

"Dear heavenly Father, when weariness begins to outlast
grace, heaviness feels more daily than hope, and things we
thought would change for the better continue a downward
spiral, where can we go but to you? Father, we crave your
heart-renewing, perspective-giving, thirst-satisfying presence
... Father, you know all the details of our broken stories and
aching hearts; what we know is that you are good, that you
can be trusted, and that hope is the order of this day."[32]

---

32 Scotty Smith, *Every Season Prayers: Gospel-Centered Prayers for the Whole of*

"*Jesus said, 'I thirst,' and herein He gave permission to all of you who are bowed down with your griefs and your sorrows to whisper them into the ears of those who watch by the bed, and to say, 'I thirst'. I daresay you have often felt ashamed of yourselves for this. You have said, 'Now, if I had some huge trouble, or if the pangs I suffered were absolutely mortal, I could lean upon the Beloved's arm. But as for this ache, or this pain, it darts through my body and causes me much anguish, though it does not kill me…' Well, but just as Jesus wept that He might let you weep on account of your sorrows and your griefs, so He says, 'I thirst,' that you might have permission patiently, as He did, to express your little complaints, that you might not think He sneers at you, or looks down upon you as though you were an alien, that you might know He sympathises with you in it all.*"

Charles Spurgeon, "The Saviour's Thirst", Sermon #3385

Life (Baker Publishing, 2016), p 154-156.

CHAPTER 39

"It is finished"

READ JOHN 19:30

*O*f all the possible adjectives, why is it that for thousands of years since the bloody and gruesome murder of Jesus on the cross, Christians have designated this particular Friday as "good" Friday? Because of three profound words, cried out in the final moments of Jesus' life before he died.

"It is finished."

What is three words in English is only one in the original Greek, in which John wrote his Gospel: *tetelestai*. Charles Spurgeon describes this word as "an ocean of meaning in a drop of language ... it would need all the other words that ever were spoken, or ever can be spoken, to explain this one word. It is altogether immeasurable."[33]

"It is finished."

What exactly did Jesus finish?

He finished the work the Father had given him—for us—with nothing left undone. He finished the requirements the law demanded—for us—with no blemish or spot in his

---

33 Charles Spurgeon, "Christ's Dying Word for His Church", Sermon #2344.

obedience. He finished the cup of God's judgment—for us—absorbing it all and spilling not a drop. He finished atoning for sin—our sin—paying the penalty in full with his blood. The cry of Jesus in his final breaths was not one of despair but of triumph.

Consider the scope of what Jesus has accomplished in full for all who believe! Love has been revealed. Wrath has been absorbed. Debt has been cleared. Condemnation has been cancelled. Satan has been conquered. Prophecy has been fulfilled. Enemies have been reconciled. Rebels have been pardoned. Access has been granted. Heaven has been guaranteed. What can you and I possibly add to the perfect work of Jesus?

Nothing.

Because, *it is finished.*

So go ahead and tell that to every doubt about God's love for you. *It is finished.*

Tell it to every anxiety that he might change his mind about you. *It is finished.*

Preach it to every fear you harbour that he is holding out on you. *It is finished.*

All has been taken care of. And what our great and gracious Saviour requires of you is to come to him and rest in that finished work that he has completely accomplished for you. In a powerful poem about the greatest sacrifice of all, D.A. Carson shows just how completely and gloriously Christ has triumphed through his death.

> *"On that wretched day the soldiers mocked him,*
> *Raucous laughter in a barracks room,*
> *'Hail the king!' they sneered, while spitting on him,*
> *Brutal beatings on this day of gloom.*
> *Though his crown was thorn, he was born a king—*
> *Holy brilliance bathed in bleeding loss—*

All the soldiers blind to this stunning theme:
Jesus reigning from a cursed cross.

"Awful weakness mars the battered God-man,
Far too broken now to hoist the beam.
Soldiers strip him bare and pound the nails in,
Watch him hanging on the cruel tree.
God's own temple's down! He has been destroyed!
Death's remains are laid in rock and sod.
But the temple rises in God's wise ploy:
Our great temple is the Son of God.

"Here's the one who says he cares for others,
One who says he came to save the lost.
How can we believe that he saves others
When he can't get off that bloody cross?
'Let him save himself! Let him come down now!'—
Savage jeering at the King's disgrace.
But by hanging there is precisely how
Christ saves others as the King of grace.

"Draped in darkness, utterly rejected,
Crying, 'Why have you forsaken me?'
Jesus bears God's wrath alone, dejected—
Weeps the bitt'rest tears instead of me.
All the mockers cry, 'He has lost his trust!
He's defeated by hypocrisy!'
But with faith's resolve, Jesus knows he must
Do God's will and swallow death for me."[34]

It is finished indeed. And that's why Christians call this
Friday "good".

---

34 D.A. Carson, *Scandalous: The Cross and Resurrection of Jesus* (Crossway, 2010), p 36-37.

REFLECT

Meditate on Carson's words above and on how deep the love of Jesus is for you.

*"Yes, glorious Lamb of God, it is finished! You have been tempted in all points like as we are, yet have You sinned in none! It **was** finished, for the last arrow out of Satan's quiver had been shot at You. The last blasphemous insinuation, the last wicked temptation had spent its fury on You. The prince of this world had surveyed You from head to foot, within and without, but he had found nothing in You. Now, your trial is over, You have finished the work which Your Father gave You to do, and so finished it that hell itself cannot accuse You of a flaw. And now, looking upon Your entire obedience, You say, "It is finished," and we Your people believe most joyously that it is even so."*

Charles Spurgeon, "It Is Finished!", Sermon #421

CHAPTER 40

(*Silence*)

READ JOHN 19:38-42

I find the silence of Holy Saturday deafening.

The torrential downpour of words from Jesus on Thursday (John 13 – 17) slowed to a few scattered raindrops on Friday. And by Saturday, the heavens had closed up.

As the final cry of *"It is finished"* escaped his lips, Jesus gave up his spirit and spoke no more.

The Word, who "was in the beginning with God" (John 1:2), had stopped speaking.

The Voice that called forth Lazarus from the grave had fallen silent.

The Author of life had laid aside his pen, his mouth sealed shut like the tomb in which he lay.

Silence.

No more will we hear his voice, thought the disciples, numb with despair.

No more will we hear his voice, rejoiced the Pharisees, and all of hell.

Silence.

"My God, my God, why have you forsaken me?" (Mark 15:34).

Silence.

"For whatever the Father does, that the Son does likewise," said Jesus in John 5:19.

And when Jesus was on the cross, the Father had been silent. So now the Son was likewise silent.

Silence.

That's the haunting soundtrack of Holy Saturday. The world turns round on its axis again, in the quiet aftermath of the death of God. Jesus endured the silence of the Father so that you and I could know the song of the resurrection.

Today is Saturday. But, it is only Saturday.

Sunday is on the way.

> *"Our God shall come, and shall not keep silent."*
>
> *(Psalm 50:3 NKJV)*

REFLECT

Spend some extended time in silence today. Feel the weight of Good Friday. Feel the hope of Resurrection Sunday. Embrace the tension, consider what Jesus has done for you and give your heart space to adore him.

> *"I would ask you to just stoop down, and in faith and love to kiss those wounds, admire that pierced hand, that other hand, that nailed foot, that other foot, that side with the spear gash, that dear face with closed eyes, and then say, 'He bore all this for me'."*

Charles Spurgeon, "A Royal Funeral", Sermon #2390

CHAPTER 41

"Peace be with you"

READ JOHN 20:1-21

*J*ohn in this chapter wants you to be convinced of two things:

1) That he was definitely faster than Peter (John 20:4).
2) That Jesus is definitely risen.

As Mary came bursting into the place where the disciples were gathered, she could barely contain herself. They must have thought they'd misheard her. "Wait, you've seen *what?*" I can imagine one asking in disbelief. "Who did you say you've seen?" interjects another. Over and over she must have exclaimed it:

"I have seen the Lord!" (v 18)

Then, that evening, as they gathered behind a locked door, Jesus suddenly appeared in their midst. Do we really think that the angel rolled the heavy stone away from the mouth of the tomb to let Jesus out? Not even close. The stone was moved to let us in. The risen Jesus walks through walls. And here he appears—risen in glory—and says to those wondering if the greatest news their ears had ever heard was true, *"Peace be with you"* (v 19). And Mary's joy becomes their joy.

Everything in Christianity depends on the resurrection of Jesus Christ from the dead. No resurrection? No joy, for the Messiah remains dead. No forgiveness, for his payment proved to be insufficient. No hope, for "your faith is futile and you are still in your sins" (1 Corinthians 15:17), and every claim of Jesus was a lie.

But Jesus was not dead. He had risen. And he is still risen to this day!

The resurrection of Jesus declared that his payment for the debt of our sin had indeed been accepted. The resurrection of Jesus announced the defeat of Satan and the funeral of death. He has done it all! For Jesus is the Prince of Peace, and the peace that he gives will never come to an end (Isaiah 9:6-7). And now that the disciples had seen the Lord, this peace was theirs.

Have you seen the Lord? Has the Holy Spirit poured resurrection life into your heart so that you come towards God in trust instead of running from him in defiance? Then the peace that only Jesus can give is yours. As I've written elsewhere, "In Christ you have a future that nothing in this world can give you and nothing in this world can take away from you. Death can't even scratch you [because] your future is resurrection."[35]

So go ahead and rejoice today! Sing loud your hallelujahs and "smile big" like an idiot! Raise your voice with millions around the world who have entered into peace with God, because Christ has indeed been raised from the grave.

PRAY

Lord Jesus, you are risen indeed! My worst day is behind me. My resurrection is ahead of me. My sins are forgiven, and my future is sure. I praise you that you do indeed give life to all who believe in you. Jesus, I believe. And even as I rejoice in the resurrection life you have poured into my heart through

---

35 Adam Ramsey, *Truth on Fire: Gazing at God Until Your Heart Sings* (The Good Book Company, 2021), p 162.

the Holy Spirit, I know that there is yet unspeakably more to come. Amen!

"As it was at the beginning of our Saviour's life, so it was at the end, for this was our Lord's legacy to all His disciples: 'Peace I leave with you, my peace I give unto you'. That which gives one of His titles even to God Himself—for He is called 'the God of peace'—should be very precious to your soul. Peace is the fit result of what the Saviour has done for you. Has He forgiven you? Then you have peace. Has He saved you? Oh then, feel an inward peace which none can take from you! Did He die for you? Then you can never die, in the full meaning of the word, so be at rest about that matter. Has He risen for you? Then, because He lives, you shall live also, so, let not your heart be troubled, but be at peace. Will He come again to receive you unto Himself? Oh, then, let your peace be like a river flowing from the very throne of God! ... Your greatest sorrows are over, your heaviest burdens Christ has carried, the most terrible disaster that could ever happen to you has been averted by Him, the most fearful calamity that you once had cause to dread can never come to you. You are an heir of God, and a joint heir with Jesus Christ. You shall have all you really need in this life, and you shall have the heaven of God in the life to come."

Charles Spurgeon, "Go in Peace", Sermon #2770

CHAPTER 42

"Do you love me?"

READ JOHN 21:15-19

*J*ust as this book began with a question (*What are you seeking?*), here we close with one. After breakfast on the beach, Jesus looks at Peter and gets right to the heart of things. The risen Jesus does not ask questions that he does not already know the answer to. He's not asking for his own sake but for Peter's. And for ours.

"Simon, son of John, do you love me?" (John 21:15)

What must go through Peter's mind as these words cut deep into his heart? The Lord does not address him now as Peter (or Cephas)—the name he gave him back in John 1:42, meaning "the rock". He addresses him as "Simon, son of John". A few days earlier, when Jesus had been on trial for his life, Peter had also faced questions—from a slave girl. And Peter, the so-called "rock," had crumbled. He denied even knowing Jesus. Three times. So how painfully humbling it must be for Peter to hear Jesus refer to him now just as "Simon". Yet how necessary. Graciously and gently, like an expert surgeon, Jesus is cutting away with each question any remnants of self-trust and self-righteousness that might remain in Peter. And on this third time, Peter, grieved to the bone, replies:

"Lord, you know everything; you know that I love you."

(John 21:17)

Three times Peter denied him. Three times Jesus questioned him. Three times Peter said, *Yes, Lord, you know I do*. After each response, Jesus reminded Peter to feed and tend to his sheep. His people. Those he had given his life for.

Without love for Jesus, nothing else matters. It is entirely possible to regularly attend church, read the Bible, sing loudly, give generously, achieve greatly and sacrifice constantly… and not truly love Jesus. You can have perfect theology, and yet lack love for Jesus. Our friend and guide through this book, Charles Spurgeon, reminds us, "What is orthodoxy without love, but a catacomb to bury dead religion in? It is a cage without a bird, the gaunt skeleton of a man out of which the life has fled."[36] Or, in Paul's words, "And if I have prophetic powers, and understand all mysteries and all knowledge, and if I have all faith, so as to remove mountains, but have not love, I am nothing" (1 Corinthians 13:2).

Jesus knew Peter loved him. The question, once again, was not for Jesus' sake but for Peter's. Peter needed to see himself and examine himself and even remind himself that there was no more important relationship in the world to him than one with Jesus.

And now, through his word, Jesus turns his eyes to you and me, and asks us the same:

"Do you love me?"

Let the question search you. Let it frustrate you. Let it bring you to the end of yourself. Remember, the Lord already knows the real answer. The question is, do you?

And if you do, and your heart leaps in protest that nothing in all the world could be more true and no person in the world

---

36 Charles Spurgeon, *"Lovest Thou Me?"*, Sermon #1281.

more deserving of your devotion, it is then that Jesus has two more words: *"Follow me"* (John 21:19). Jesus repeats at the end the command he gave in the beginning: *"Follow me"*.

You see, to love Jesus is to follow him. As Jesus has given himself for us, he calls his followers to give themselves unreservedly to him. To walk with him and draw near to him. To give him your trust, your obedience and your repentance when you get it wrong. To follow Jesus is to believe that he has loved you with a love vaster than the universe, and to make your home there and invite others into the joy that you have in him. *"Do you love me? … Follow me."*

And Peter did. He followed Jesus all the way to his own cross. Because he loved him. Because he knew that Jesus alone had "the words of eternal life" (6:68). And because no one was more worthy of his life—his whole life with nothing held back—than Jesus.

May this be true of us as well.

REFLECTION
"Do you love me?" Talk to Jesus with your answer.

> *"With unvarying tone and look the Lord inquired, 'Simon, son of John, do you love me?' It shows what weight our Saviour attached to the matter of his love, that He asked him about **that**, about **that only**, and about **that three times over** … You may turn over the pages of your book, you may digest doctrine after doctrine, you may take up theological propositions and problems, and you may labour to solve this difficulty and expound that text, and meet the other question, till, somehow or other, the heart grows as dry as the leaves of the volume, and the book-*

worm feeds on the soul as well as the paper, eating its way into the spirit. It is, therefore, a healthy thing for the Lord to come into the study and close the book, and say to the student, 'Sit still a while, and let Me ask you, "Do you love me?" I am better than all books and studies. Have you a warm, human, living love to Me?' I hope many of you are very diligent students—if you teach in the Sunday school you ought to be; if you preach in the streets or in cottage meetings you ought to be. How shall you fill others if you are not full yourselves? But, at the same time look most of all to the condition of your heart towards Christ. To know is good, but to love is better ... Putting all together, let me say to you—beloved, however eminent you may be in the church of God, and however distinguished for services or for suffering, yet do not evade this question. Bare your bosoms to the inspection of your Lord. Answer Him with humble boldness while He says to you again and again, even till He grieves you, 'Simon, son of John, do you love me?' ...

"Now, tomorrow, and as long as ever you live, do everything out of love to Christ. It will spread flowers over your work, and make it look beautiful in His eyes. Put love's fingers to work, love's brains, love's eyes, love's hands, think with love, pray with love, speak with love, live with love, and in this way you will live with power, and God will bless you for Jesus' sake. Amen."

Charles Spurgeon, "Lovest Thou Me?", Sermon #1281